CONTEMPORARY'S

Make Your Mark
in Food Service

PHYLLIS POGRUND
ROSEMARY GREBEL

CONTEMPORARY BOOKS

a division of NTC/CONTEMPORARY PUBLISHING GROUP
Lincolnwood, Illinois USA

ISBN: 0-8092-0907-1

Published by Contemporary Books,
a division of NTC/Contemporary Publishing Group, Inc.,
4255 West Touhy Avenue,
Lincolnwood (Chicago), Illinois 60646-1975 U.S.A.

Director, New Product Development
Noreen Lopez

Editorial Manager
Cynthia Krejcsi

Project Manager
Laurie Duncan

Editorial
Carlos Byfield

Design and Production Manager
Norma Underwood

Cover Design
Michael Kelly

Production Artist
Kristy Sheldon

Line Art Illustrations
David Will

Contents

Dear Student,

Welcome to *Make Your Mark in Food Service*. This book can open the door to a world of employment opportunities for you. Food service is one of the fastest growing industries today, and with that growth comes a demand for workers with the right skills.

In this book, you will learn the vocabulary and information needed to perform a job in the food service business. You will
- practice actual conversations that you can use on the job.
- learn how to talk to a manager and to co-workers.
- discover how to work cooperatively for success as a team member.
- find out what it takes to become a manager.

We hope that this book gives you a head start in preparing yourself for future entry into the job market. We wish you much success.

Phyllis Pogrund
Rosemary Grebel

Unit 1
FOR HERE OR TO GO?

Look at the picture. Which words from the box below are pictured?
What job does the woman have? What is the man doing?

Words to Know:

apple pie	French fries	restaurant	(to) drink	Come again.
beverage	hamburger	salad	(to) eat	Excuse me.
cheeseburger	ice cream	sandwich		For here or
chicken	juice	side order	large	to go?
coffee	ketchup	size	low fat	Of course.
cookie	knife	soda	medium	Over there.
counter	milk	soft drink	orange	Thank you.
customer	napkin	spoon	small	Welcome to . . .
dessert	onion	straw		You're
dressing	onion rings	tax	certainly	welcome.
fish	order	tea	please	
fork	pickle	worker	Anything	
			else?	

Listen and Speak

Step 1: Listen as your teacher reads the dialogue.

Kim: Welcome to A-1 Burgers. May I take your order?

Customer: Yes, please. I want a cheeseburger, no onions or pickles. I want a large order of French fries and a salad with low fat dressing.

Kim: Anything to drink?

Customer: Oh yes, an orange soda.

Kim: What size?

Customer: Medium.

Kim: Anything else?

Customer: Yes. Coffee.

Kim: For here or to go?

Customer: To go.

Kim: That will be $5.79 with tax. Thank you.

LATER

Customer: Excuse me. May I have some ketchup?

Kim: Yes. Here you are.

Customer: And may I have a spoon and a fork?

Kim: Of course. Here you are.

Customer: Oh, and a knife, too.

Kim: Certainly. Here you are.

Customer: And where are the napkins?

Kim: On the end of the counter. Over there.

Customer: Thank you.

Kim: You're welcome. Thank *you*. Come again.

Step 2: Work with a partner.
Practice the dialogue.

Step 3: Talk about Kim.
Is she a good worker?
Why do you think so?

Menu

SANDWICHES

hamburger	$1.75
cheeseburger	$1.99
chicken sandwich	$1.75
fish sandwich	$1.60

BEVERAGES

milk	$ .75
coffee	$ .50
tea	$ .50
orange juice	$1.00
soft drinks	
small	$ .80
medium	$ .90
large	$1.00

SIDE ORDERS

salad	$ .99
French fries	
small	$ .75
medium	$1.00
large	$1.25
onion rings	$1.00

DESSERTS

cookie	$ .50
ice cream	$1.35
apple pie	$ .99

You are a worker in a fast-food restaurant. Write on the lines to complete the conversation. Then read the complete conversation with a partner.

You: May I take your order?

Customer: Yes. I want _____

and _____.

You: Anything else?

Customer: Yes. I want _____.

You: Anything else?

Customer: _____.

You: For here or to go?

Customer: _____.

Build Your Vocabulary

Step 1: Read the words in the box.

Step 2: Work with a partner.
Take turns reading the questions and answers.

Customer: May I have **a straw?**   OR   May I have **some straws?**

             a knife?   **some knives?**

             a cup?   **some cups?**

             a lid?   **some lids?**

             a small plate?   **some small plates?**

Worker: Here you are.

Customer: May I have **some mustard?**

                some mayonnaise?

                some creamer?

                some salt and pepper?

Worker: Here you are.

Customer: Where **is the ketchup?**   Where **are the napkins?**

          Where **is the salt?**   Where **are the cups?**

          Where **is the pepper?**   Where **are the stir sticks?**

          Where **is the sugar?**   Where **are the forks?**

Worker: Over there, at the end of the counter.

Step 3: Fill in the spaces below. Then practice with a partner.

Customer: May I have a _____?   May I have some _____?

Worker: Here you are.

Customer: Where is the _____?   Where are the _____?

Worker: Over there, at the end of the counter.

Write the correct word from the word list under the picture.

creamer	knife	napkin	spoon
cup	lid	pepper	stir stick
fork	mayonnaise	plate	straw
ketchup	mustard	salt	sugar

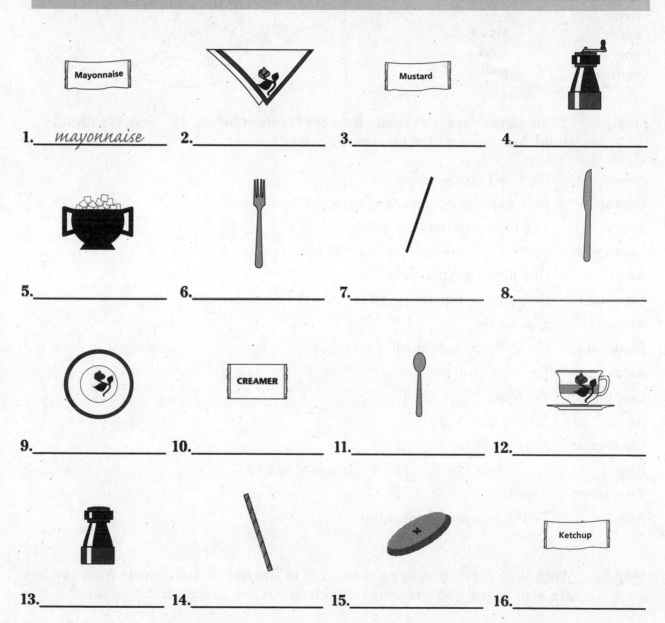

1. _mayonnaise_   2. _____   3. _____   4. _____

5. _____   6. _____   7. _____   8. _____

9. _____   10. _____   11. _____   12. _____

13. _____   14. _____   15. _____   16. _____

Listen and Speak

Words to Know:

bag
cash register
change
counter person
diet cola
price
refill
tray
uniform

(to) cost
(to) make eye
  contact
(to) smile

clean
free
polite

Step 1: Listen as your teacher reads the conversation below. The conversation is about Anna, a counter person at Speedy Foods.

Anna:	Hi. May I take your order?
Customer:	How much does a piece of apple pie cost?
Anna:	The price is ninety-five cents.
Customer:	May I have three pieces of apple pie?
Anna:	Of course. Anything else?
Customer:	Do you give free drink refills?
Anna:	Yes, we do.
Customer:	Good. I want one small diet cola.
Anna:	For here or to go?
Customer:	For here.
Anna:	That will be $3.92.
Customer:	Here is $5.
Anna:	Okay. Your change is $1.08. Here is your tray.
Customer:	Thank you.
Anna:	Thank *you*, and come again!

Step 2: Work with a partner. Read the words in the box. Which words from the box are also in the conversation? Which words are shown in the picture?

Step 3: Practice the conversation with a partner.

Step 4: Discuss these questions with your partner:
- How does Anna find the cost of the order?
- Is Anna polite to the customers? How do you know?

Practice

Draw a line from each picture to the correct words on the right.

1.

    a. Anna uses the cash register to find the cost of the order.

2.

    b. Anna asks the customer for an order.

3.

    c. Anna tells the customer the price of the order.

4.

    d. If the customer wants the food to go, Anna puts the food in a bag.

5.

    e. If the customer wants to eat in the restaurant, Anna puts the food on a tray.

Circle *Yes* or *No* for each sentence below.

1. Anna is a customer in a fast-food restaurant.   **Yes**   **No**

2. Anna uses a cash register to find the cost of the order.   **Yes**   **No**

3. If the customer wants the food to go, Anna puts it in her napkin.   **Yes**   **No**

4. If the customer wants to eat in the restaurant, Anna puts the food on a tray.   **Yes**   **No**

Be a Good Worker

Step 1: Look at the big picture. Sara is watching a videotape for new employees at the City Burger restaurant. She also has the list of rules below. What rules from the list does the worker on the videotape follow?

RULES FOR NEW WORKERS

1. Smile and make eye contact with the customers. Always be polite.

2. Remember to shower and to wear a clean uniform.

3. Never eat, drink, or smoke on the job.

4. Keep your nails short and clean.

5. Cover or tie back long hair.

6. Don't waste time. Clean your work area or help another worker when you aren't busy.

Step 2: Look at the small picture. It is Sara's first day of work. Which rules is she following? Which rules does she still need to learn?

Have Some Fun!

Use the words in the box to fill in the spaces in the puzzle.

cheeseburger	medium	salad
counter	order	small
large	pie	uniform
low fat	refill	worker

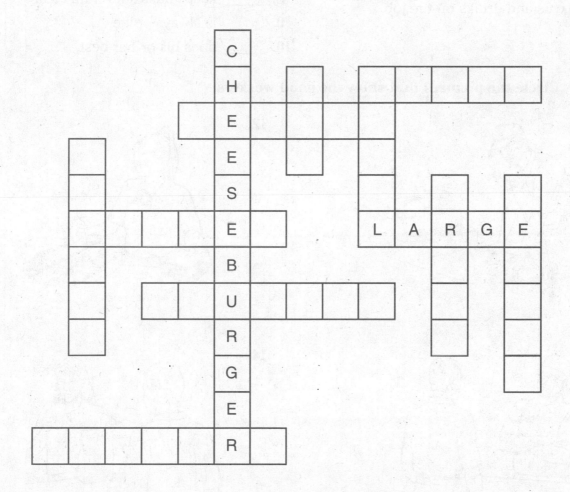

Think It Over

Step 1: What does a good worker do? Put a check next to the words that tell what a good worker does.

A good worker

1. _____ smiles at customers.
2. _____ smokes on the job.
3. _____ covers or pulls back long hair.
4. _____ wastes time.
5. _____ eats and drinks on the job.

6. _____ showers and wears a clean uniform.
7. _____ doesn't make eye contact with customers.
8. _____ keeps nails short and clean.
9. _____ is always polite.
10. _____ does his or her best.

Step 2: Circle the pictures that show the good workers.

11.

12.

13.

14.

Check Your Understanding

Step 1: For each question, circle the letter of the best answer.

The worker asks:

1. May I take your order?

2. For here or to go?

3. Anything else?

4. What size?

The customer answers:

a. Yes, please. I want a small salad.
b. No. That will be all.

a. You're welcome.
b. For here.

a. Thank you.
b. Yes, an order of French fries.

a. That will be all.
b. Small.

Step 2: For each question, circle the letter of the best answer.

The customer asks:

1. Where are the napkins?

2. May I have some extra ketchup?

3. Excuse me. May I have a spoon?

The worker answers:

a. Thank you. Come again.
b. On the end of the counter.

a. Yes. Here you are.
b. You're welcome.

a. Certainly.
b. No.

Step 3: Underline the words a polite worker uses.

Complete activity 1, 2, or 3. Then do activity 4 on your own.
Write your answers on other paper.

1. Go to two fast-food restaurants. Compare the menus with the menu on page 3 of this book. Answer the following questions.
   - Are the prices the same?
   - Do they offer the same foods?

2. Work with a small group of students. Talk about your favorite fast-food restaurant.
   - Do you like the same fast-food restaurant?
   - What does each student like about his or her favorite fast-food restaurant?
   - How do the workers treat the customers at each restaurant?

3. Find out how much workers earn working in a fast-food restaurant near you.
   - How much is the minimum wage in your state?
   - Is the minimum wage different from the restaurant wage?

4. Ask yourself the following questions about good working habits.
   - What does a good worker do?
   - Do I have good work habits? What are my good work habits?

Notes

_____

_____

_____

_____

_____

Unit 2
DRIVE UP TO THE WINDOW

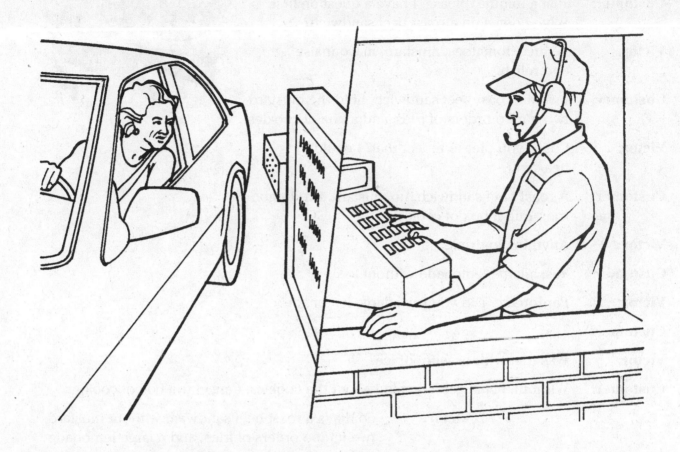

Study the picture. What is the woman saying? What is the man doing?
What words from the box help you answer these questions?

Words to Know:

box	(to) cancel	cold	Did you say . . . ?
ice	(to) drive up	correct	Hold the . . .
lemonade	(to) hear	hot	How about . . . ?
lettuce	(to) order	jumbo	I changed my
relish	(to) repeat	ready	mind.
roast beef			Just a minute.
tomatoes	could	with	Pardon me.
window	couldn't	without	That's all.
			Was that . . . ?
			What comes
			on . . . ?

Listen and Speak

Step 1: Listen as your teacher reads the dialogue.

Victor: Welcome to A–1 Burgers. Are you ready to order?

Customer: Just a minute, please. I have a question first. What comes on a roast beef sandwich?

Victor: Lettuce, tomatoes, mustard, mayonnaise, and relish.

Customer: I want a roast beef sandwich, hold the mustard, two jumbo orders of fries, and a box of cookies.

Victor: Could you please repeat that? I couldn't hear you.

Customer: A roast beef sandwich, no mustard, two jumbo fries, and a box of cookies.

Victor: Anything to drink?

Customer: Yes, a large lemonade without ice.

Victor: Pardon me. Did you say a large lemonade?

Customer: Yes.

Victor: Was that with or without ice?

Customer: Without. I changed my mind about the cookies. Cancel the box of cookies.

Victor: So that's a roast beef sandwich without mustard, two jumbo orders of fries, and a large lemonade without ice. Is that correct?

Customer: Correct.

Victor: How about a piece of hot apple pie, too?

Customer: No, thanks, that's all.

Victor: That will be $7.85. Please drive up to the first window. Thank you.

Step 2: Work with a partner. Practice the dialogue.

Step 3: Talk about the conversation. Discuss these questions:
- **Why does Victor ask questions about the order?**
- **What does the customer want to know about the roast beef sandwich? Why?**
- **Why does Victor talk about a piece of hot apple pie?**

Practice

Draw a line from the restaurant order to the correct picture.

1. I want a lemonade.

a.

2. We want two orders of onion rings.

b.

3. The customers want three salads.

c.

You are a worker in a fast-food restaurant. Write on the lines to complete the conversation. Then read the complete conversation with a partner.

You: Welcome to A–1 Burgers. Are you ready to order?

Customer: Yes. I want an order of fries and a chicken sandwich.

You: _____

Customer: Yes. A large lemonade with lots of ice.

You: Was that _____?

Customer: Large.

You: So that's _____ and

_____?

Customer: Correct.

You: _____?

Customer: No, thanks. That's all.

You: That will be _____.

Thank you.

Build Your Vocabulary

Step 1: Read the paragraph below.

Victor works at the drive-through window at A–1 Burgers. He takes orders from customers. Usually they are in a hurry. They want their food right away. They do not like to wait. Victor works fast. He listens carefully. He repeats the orders to the customers. The customers get the correct orders. The customers are satisfied.

Step 2: Circle the sentences that are correct.

1. Victor works fast.
2. He works slowly.
3. He listens carefully.
4. The customers are satisfied.

5. The customers like to wait.
6. They are in a hurry.
7. They don't like to get the correct orders.
8. He gives the customers the correct orders.

Keep the Customer Satisfied

Step 1: Read the paragraph below.

The customer at the counter said to Victor, "This sandwich tastes funny. This whole meal smells bad." Victor said, "I'm sorry. Can I get you something else?" Victor wanted to keep the customer satisfied.

Step 2: Write a *V* next to the words that Victor says.
Write a *C* next to the words the customer says.

1. _____ Are you ready to order?
2. _____ I'm sorry. Can I get you something else?
3. _____ This meal tastes funny.

4. _____ Cancel that order.
5. _____ I changed my mind.
6. _____ Anything to drink?

Practice

Complete the dialogues below. Use the pictures at the right to help you.
Then practice each dialogue with a partner.

1. **Worker:**   Are you ready to order?

   Customer: Yes, I want _one roast beef_
   sandwich, one box of cookies, and a cup
   of coffee.

2. **Worker:**   Is your friend ready to order?

   Customer: Yes, she wants _____

   _____

   _____

3. **Worker:**   Are you ready to order?

   Customer: Yes. We want _____

   _____

   _____

4. **Worker:**   Are you ready to order?

   Customer: Yes. I want _____

   _____

   _____

5. **Worker:**   Are your children ready to order?

   Customer: Yes. They want _____

   _____

   _____

Listen and Speak

Step 1: Listen as your teacher reads the telephone conversation.

Minh: Hello. Mama Mia's Pizza. Can you hold, please?

LATER

Minh: Thank you for holding. May I help you?

Caller: Yes. Is your large pizza enough for four people?

Minh: Yes, it's enough for four or five people. There are ten slices.

Caller: OK. I want a large cheese pizza with a thick crust and an order of garlic bread. I have a coupon.

Minh: Is that for pick-up or delivery?

Caller: Delivery.

Minh: May I have your name and address, please?

Caller: This is Robert Lee at 123 South Main Street, Sur City.

Words to Know:	
address	slices
apartment	veggie/
avenue	vegetable
caller	topping
cheese	
coupon	(to) call
cross street	(to) deliver
crust	(to) hold
delivery	(to) pay
diameter	(to) pick up
driver	(to) understand
garlic bread	
house	enough
mushroom	extra
pepperoni	near/nearest
phone number	thick
pick-up	
pizza	That will be
sausage	about . . .

Minh: Is that a house or an apartment?

Caller: A house.

Minh: May I have your phone number, please?

Caller: 555-4429.

Minh: What's the nearest big cross street?

Caller: Pine Avenue.

Minh: So, that's a large cheese pizza with a thick crust and an order of garlic bread delivered to 123 S. Main Street in Sur City. Your phone number is 555-4429. Will that be all?

Caller: Yes, thanks.

Minh: That will be about forty-five minutes. Please pay the driver $13.52. Thank you for calling Mama Mia's Pizza. Good-bye.

Step 2: Read the telephone conversation with a partner.

Step 1: Put a check mark next to what Minh does at work.

1. She says, "Hello. Mama Mia's Pizza."   (√)

2. She takes orders from customers.   (   )

3. She never says, "Please."   (   )

4. She repeats the orders.   (   )

5. She asks, "Is that for pick-up or delivery?"   (   )

6. She never takes orders from callers.   (   )

7. She asks questions about the orders.   (   )

8. She never asks callers for their telephone numbers.   (   )

9. She never tells the customers how much to pay.   (   )

10. She says, "Thank you."   (   )

Step 2: Match each question with an answer. The first one is done for you.

1. Is that for pick-up or delivery?   **a.** 447 First Drive, Longton.

2. May I have your address, please?   **b.** Yes.

3. Is that a house or an apartment?   **c.** 555-4429.

4. May I have your phone number, please?   **d.** Delivery.

5. What's the nearest big cross street?   **e.** Pine Avenue.

6. Will that be all?   **f.** A house.

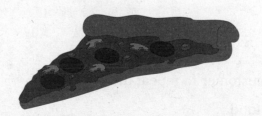

Be a Good Worker

Step 1: Look at the pictures and read the questions that Victor and Minh ask. Victor and Minh ask questions because they want the customers to get the correct order. Sometimes the two workers repeat what they think the customer said. Other times they ask the customer to repeat the order.

Victor: Did you say with or without ice?
Was that *two* orders of fries?

Minh: Could you please repeat that?
I couldn't hear you.
Did you say a *small* pizza?

Sometimes Victor and Minh ask the customer for more information. Here are some questions they might ask:

- Is that a house or an apartment?
- Is that for pick-up or delivery?
- Anything to drink?

Step 2: Fill in the spaces below with the correct words.

Could you please _____ that? I couldn't _____ you.

Did you _____ a small or a large salad? Was _____

one or two cups of coffee?

Step 3: Put the sentences in order from 1 to 6.

_____ **1.** The worker asks the customer to repeat the order.

_____ **2.** The customer orders food.

_____ **3.** The worker gives the customer the food.

_____ **4.** The worker says, "Are you ready to order?"

_____ **5.** The customer repeats the order.

_____ **6.** The worker doesn't hear or understand the order.

Have Some Fun!

Find the underlined words on the menu. Then look for the underlined words in the puzzle below. The words may be horizontal, vertical, or diagonal. They may even be backwards! Circle the words you find in the puzzle. Then find and circle these extra words: crust, pan, pie, piece, slices.

Mama Mia's Pizza

SIZE	MINI	SMALL	MEDIUM	LARGE
Diameter	8"	11"	13"	15"
Cheese only	3.14	6.34	7.97	9.87
Extra topping	.75	.90	1.15	1.25
Veggie	6.54	9.27	11.54	13.97
Mama's special	6.97	10.27	12.54	15.51
Half and half	6.97	10.27	12.54	15.51
All meat	7.12	11.34	13.87	16.97
The works	n/a	11.97	14.74	18.21

TOPPINGS

Spicy Pepperoni Sausage Mushrooms Onions Extra Cheese
Green Peppers Black Olives Pineapple Canadian Bacon
Salami Anchovies Ground Beef Spinach Sliced Tomato

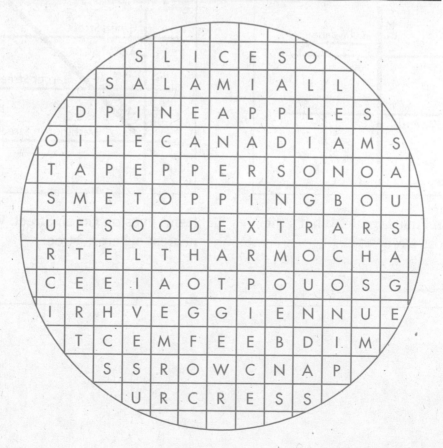

Answer each question below.

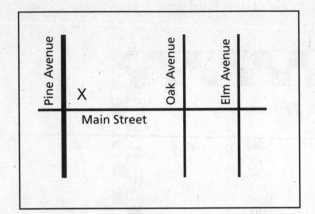

Marie lives on Main Street. The nearest big street is Pine Avenue. What's the nearest big cross street?

1. _____Pine Avenue_____

3. _____

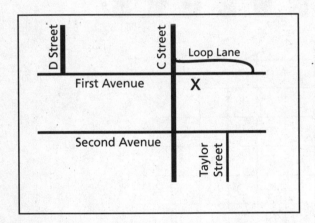

Teresa lives on First Avenue. What's the nearest big cross street?

2. _____

Razmik lives on Ocean Avenue. What's the nearest big cross street?

Henri lives on Green Street. What's the nearest big cross street?

4. _____

Check Your Understanding

You are taking orders at Mama Mia's Pizza. Fill in the missing parts of the conversation below. Then read the complete conversation with a partner.

You: Mama Mia's Pizza. May I help you?

Caller: Yes. I want a medium veggie pizza with extra cheese.

You: Is that for _____?

Caller: Delivery.

You: May I have your _____?

Caller: Maria Santana at 39 Fig St., Apartment B, Middleton Gardens.

You: Did you say _____?

Caller: Yes, that's correct.

You: May I have your _____?

Caller: 555-1122.

You::   Did you say _____?

Caller: Yes, that's right.

You: What's the nearest _____?

Caller: Orange Street.

You: So, that's _____

_____

_____?

Caller: Yes.

You: That will be _____

_____

_____.

Try It!

Complete the first three activities in class. Then do activity 4 or 5 on your own. Write your answers on other paper.

1. Draw a map that shows the street where you live. Include the nearest cross street.

2. Work with a small group of students. Ask students for their addresses and the nearest cross streets to their homes. Then write their addresses.

3. Work with a partner. Practice ordering a pizza on the telephone. Your partner will be the restaurant worker. Then change roles and practice again.

4. Call in an order to a local pizza restaurant. Write down the questions the worker asks you. Which questions were the same as the questions on page 18? Which questions were different?

5. Go to a drive-through window at a fast-food restaurant. Order something from the menu. Does the worker repeat your order or ask questions about it? Does the worker get your order right?

Notes

_____

_____

_____

_____

_____

_____

_____

Unit 3
HOW WOULD YOU LIKE YOUR STEAK?

Read the words in the box. What words are pictured above? What are the people in the picture talking about?

Words to Know:

appetizer	ma'am	soup	(to) see	Enjoy your
baked potato	meal	sour cream	(to) serve	meal.
bits	oil	special		Good evening.
butter	rice	steak	another	How would
caper	rush	tonight	delicious	you like . . . ?
chef	salad dressing	waiter	rare	I'd like . . .
chives	(blue cheese,	wine	T-bone	I'll have . . .
chunk	low fat,		well-done	On the side.
decaf	Italian,			What would
halibut	ranch,	(to) begin with		you like . . . ?
herbs	Thousand	(to) cook	barely	
	Island)	(to) drop	inside	
iced tea	sauce	(to) enjoy	outside	
kind	server	(to) prepare		

Listen and Speak

Step 1: **Listen as your teacher reads the conversation.**

Max: Good evening, ma'am. I'm Max, your server. Our special tonight is Alaskan halibut with butter caper sauce. Would you like an appetizer to begin with?

Customer: No, thank you. I'll have a T-bone steak, and please bring some steak sauce.

Max: Certainly. How would you like your steak cooked?

Customer: I'd like it medium rare.

Max: Would you like a baked potato or rice with that?

Customer: I'd like a baked potato with sour cream and chives.

Max: Would you like soup or salad?

Customer: Salad, please.

Max: What kind of salad dressing would you like?

Customer: I'll have blue cheese dressing on the side.

Max: Would you like wine with your dinner?

Customer: No, thanks. I'll have a glass of water and decaf later.

Max: Anything else, ma'am?

Customer: No, thank you, waiter. But I am in a hurry.

Max: I'll bring your salad right away, and I'll put a rush on the steak.

LATER

Max: Here's your steak. Please be careful. The plate is very hot.
Enjoy your meal.
Oh, I see you dropped your fork. Here's another one.
Can I get you anything else?

Customer: No, thanks. That will be fine. The meal looks very good.

Max: Well, I hope you enjoy it.

Step 2: **Work with a partner. Practice the conversation out loud.**

Step 3: **Circle any words that you don't know. Then read the conversation again. Look for information that helps you understand the words.**

Practice

Step 1:   Read the information about steaks and salad dressing.

A Chef can prepare a steak many ways:

- Rare–the outside is brown, but the inside is bright red
- Medium rare–the outside is brown, but the inside is pink
- Medium–the outside is brown, and the inside is barely pink
- Medium well–the outside and the inside are brown
- Well–the outside is dark brown or black, and the inside is very brown

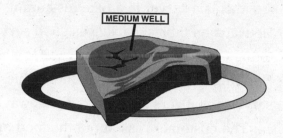

A salad usually comes with a steak. Here are descriptions of some common salad dressings:

- Ranch–White
- Thousand Island–Pink
- Blue Cheese–White with small chunks of blue cheese
- Italian–Gold with bits of herbs and pepper
- Low fat–Contains less oil or mayonnaise than regular dressing

Step 2:   Fill in the conversation below and practice with a partner.

Server: Hello. Are you ready to _____?

Customer: Yes. I'd like a _____.

Server: How would you like your steak _____?

Customer: _____ medium.

Server: _____ soup or salad?

Customer: _____ salad.

Server: What kind of salad dressing _____?

Customer: I'd like _____.

Server: Would you like anything else?

Customer: No, thanks. That will be all.

Build Your Vocabulary

Look at the pictures and read the story. Then do the exercises on the next page.

Max is a server in a nice restaurant. He waits on tables. Max gives good service to the customers. He fills their water glasses. He brings rolls and butter to their tables. He serves appetizers and drinks right away.

The customers ask about the food on the menu. Max answers their questions. He always is polite. Max also tells his customers about the specials. They are special dishes the cooks made that day. The specials change every day.

Max takes the orders from his customers. He gives the orders to the cooks. When the food is ready, Max puts a lemon or parsley garnish on the plates. Now the food looks delicious and ready to serve.

Max serves the food and then checks on the customers. He asks, "Do you want more coffee, hot water for tea, or rolls?" Then he says, "Enjoy your meal." After the customers eat, Max takes their plates. He asks, "Would you like anything else? Can I show you our dessert tray?"

Words to Know:	
break	roll
cash	service
check	tip
cook	water glass
credit card	
garnish	(to) check on
lemon	(to) relax
parsley	(to) wait on

When the customers are ready, Max brings the check. The customers pay with cash or a credit card. If they like the service, they leave a tip.

Max says "Good-bye" to the customers. He tells them, "Thank you, and come again!"

Max works hard. When he has a break, he relaxes. He reads a newspaper and has a good meal.

Practice

Step 1:   Fill in the spaces below with words from the box.

fills	service
restaurant	server
right away	serves
rolls	specials

1. Max is a _____ in a nice

    _____. Max gives good

    _____ to the customers.

    He _____ their water glasses.

    He brings _____ and butter to

    their tables. Max tells customers about the

    _____. He

    _____ appetizers and drinks

    _____.

checks on	garnish
cooks	plates
delicious	ready
dessert	serve
else	want
Enjoy your meal	tea

2. Max gives the orders to the

    _____. When the orders are

    _____, he puts a

    _____ on the plates. The food

    looks _____ and ready

to _____. Max _____ the customers. He asks if they

_____ more coffee, hot water for _____, or rolls.

He says, "_____." After the customers eat, Max takes their

_____ and asks if they would like anything _____.

He offers _____.

Step 2:   Circle *True* or *False* for each sentence.

1. Max is a cook in a nice restaurant.	**True**	**False**
2. Max tells his customers about the specials.	**True**	**False**
3. Max doesn't bring rolls and butter to his customers.	**True**	**False**
4. Max gives the orders to the cooks.	**True**	**False**
5. The customers put garnishes on their plates.	**True**	**False**
6. The customers pay with cash or credit cards.	**True**	**False**
7. Max doesn't tell his customers about the dessert tray.	**True**	**False**

Listen and Speak

Step 1: Listen as your teacher reads the conversation. The conversation is between Emi, a waitress, and a customer.

Emi: Good evening. My name is Emi, and I'll be your server. Would you like an appetizer?

Customer: Yes. What do you recommend?

Emi: Our chicken wings are our most popular item. We also have some dinner specials tonight. The specials are crab cakes and lemon chicken.

Words to Know:

bill	rice pilaf	(to) take back
chicken wings	situation	(to) try
choice	strawberry	
clam chowder	shortcake	popular
crab cakes	waitress	salty
French onion soup		
	(to) apologize	Great
item	(to) argue	I'm sorry.
margarine	(to) come with	You talked
mistake	(to) fix	me into it!
potato skins	(to) recommend	You're right.
problem	(to) solve	

Today's Specials

DINNER*
Lemon Chicken
Crab Cakes
SOUP
Clam Chowder
French Onion

* dinner specials come with rice pilaf,
your choice of soup or salad, and fresh bread

Customer: OK, I'll have some chicken wings. What do the specials come with?

Emi: They come with rice pilaf, your choice of soup or salad, and a roll.

Customer: What kind of soup do you have?

Emi: Clam chowder or French onion.

Customer: OK. I'll have the crab cakes with clam chowder.

Emi: What would you like to drink?

Customer: Coffee, but I'll have it later. And what do you recommend for dessert?

Emi: The strawberry shortcake is our most popular dessert. It's delicious.

Customer: OK, waitress. You talked me into it!

Emi: Great! Enjoy your meal.

Step 2: Practice the conversation with a partner.

Step 3: Discuss these questions:
- What is a server? What is a waitress? What is the difference between a server and a waitress?
- Why does the customer ask Emi, "What do you recommend?"
- Serving food is an important part of Emi's job. What is another important part of her job?

Practice

Step 1: Circle the letter of the best answer.

1. Emi is a
   a. waitress.
   b. housekeeper.
   c. cook.
   d. hostess.

2. The customer wants
   a. an appetizer.
   b. a menu.
   c. a napkin.
   d. a glass of water.

3. Emi recommends
   a. lemonade.
   b. apple pie.
   c. shrimp.
   d. chicken wings.

4. The customer orders
   a. lemonade.
   b. apple pie.
   c. shrimp.
   d. chicken wings.

5. The customer also orders
   a. crab cakes.
   b. lemon chicken.
   c. steak.
   d. French onion soup.

6. Emi says the strawberry shortcake is
   a. salty.
   b. delicious.
   c. hot.
   d. good.

Step 2: Complete the conversation below. Choose order number 1, 2, or 3. Then practice the conversation with a partner. Change the order each time.

Order # 1
rare steak, baked potato with butter, salad with Italian dressing

Order # 2
lemon chichen with rice and vegetables, bean soup, white wine

Order # 3
potato skins, halibut with steamed vegetables, salad with blue cheese dressing

Server: Hello, my name is _____. I'll be your server. Are you ready to order?

Customer: Yes. I'd like _____.

Server: _____?

Customer: _____.

Server: _____?

Customer: _____.

Server: Anything else?

Customer: No, thank you, that's all.

Be a Good Worker

What does a good server say to customers? It depends on the situation.
Read about the situations on this page. If the customers are happy and
satisfied, the server can relax.

Customer: That meal was delicious.

Server: I'm glad you liked it.

Sometimes customers aren't satisfied with their order.
The server should apologize and solve the problem.

Customer 1: I asked for this steak well-done.

Server: I'm sorry. I'll take it back and have it cooked some more.

Customer 2: My soup is too salty.

Server: I'm sorry. Can I get you something else?

Customer: We ordered twenty minutes ago.

Server: I'm very sorry. I'll check on your order.

Sometimes the customers are unhappy with the bill. The server should always be
polite and check on the bill.

Customer 1: Waitress, this bill can't be right. It's much too high.

Server: I'll check it for you.

Customer 2: Excuse me. This is too much. I only had a cup of coffee.

Server: You're right. That's our mistake.

Never argue with a customer, even if you are right. It's important to try to fix a
problem and keep the customer happy!

Have Some Fun!

Place each word in the box in the correct column.

blue cheese	chives	cheese	margarine
water	butter	well-done	tea
rare	medium	medium well	
Italian	low fat	ranch	
sour cream	coffee	milk	

Salad Dressings	Steaks	Drinks	Baked Potato Toppings
_____	_____	_____	_____
_____	_____	_____	_____
_____	_____	_____	_____
_____	_____	_____	_____
_____	_____	_____	_____

Find the words from the list above in this puzzle. The words may be horizontal, vertical, or diagonal. They even may be backwards! Circle the words you find. Can you find them all?

M	C	H	E	E	S	E	R	E	T	A	W
A	E	T	H	O	U	S	A	N	D	A	E
R	E	D	U	Y	W	I	N	A	X	B	L
G	F	C	I	C	E	D	C	I	T	U	L
A	F	A	S	U	A	O	H	L	T	T	D
R	O	K	L	I	M	N	I	A	A	T	O
I	C	B	A	E	E	W	V	T	F	E	N
N	U	L	N	R	A	R	E	I	W	R	E
E	D	E	D	I	L	L	S	L	O	W	N
S	O	U	R	C	R	E	A	M	L	I	O

Think It Over

Step 1: Read the common things that customers say.
Then read how a good server responds.

1. Customers say:

"I'd like water."
"Waiter, can we have some bread?"
"There are no rolls left. We need some more."
"We need some salt. There's none on the table."

Server says:

"I'll bring some right away."

2. Customers say:

"We need one more menu."
"Another bottle of white wine, please."
"I'd like a refill on my coffee, please."
"May I have another soda?"
"I'd like another beer."

Server says:

"I'll get one for you."

3. Customers say:

"Waitress, my glass has lipstick on it."
"I dropped my fork on the floor."
"My cup is dirty."
"May I have a new napkin?"

Server says:

"I'll get you a clean one."

Step 2: Match the customer's problem with the server's response. Draw a line from what the customer says to what the server says.

What the Customer Says:	**What the Server Says:**
1. "This bill is not correct."	"I'm sorry about that. I'll check it for you."
2. "We ordered fifteen minutes ago."	"I'll get you another one right now."
3. "The dinner is delicious."	"I'm glad you're enjoying it."
4. "I need another napkin."	"I'm sorry. I'll check on your order."

Check Your Understanding

Step 1: Circle the letter of the best answer.

1. What kind of soup do you have?
   a. The halibut is very good.
   b. Strawberry shortcake
   c. Clam chowder or bean soup.

2. What does it come with?
   a. The shortcake is delicious.
   b. OK. I'll have some.
   c. It comes with soup or salad.

3. What kinds of salad dressing do you have?
   a. Ranch, blue cheese, or Italian.
   b. OK. I'll get some for you.
   c. It comes with dessert.

4. What's the special?
   a. Coffee, please.
   b. The special is halibut.
   c. That's all.

5. What do you recommend?
   a. Dessert, please.
   b. What does it come with?
   c. The bean soup is delicious.

6. May I have some hot coffee?
   a. The bread here is delicious.
   b. Certainly. I'll get some for you.
   c. OK. I'll have some.

Step 2: Read the customer's questions and the server's answers.
Then practice with a partner. Change the server's answer each time.

Customer: What do you recommend?

Server: The vegetable soup is very good.
The strawberry shortcake is our most popular dessert.
Try our steak and salad.
Try the chicken wings. They are delicious.
The potato skins are great.

Customer: What are the specials tonight?

Server: Roast chicken with wine sauce is our special.
Our special dessert is lemon pie.

Answer the questions. Write your answers on the lines below.

1. The customer drops his fork on the floor. What do you say? _____

_____

2. The customer says the coffee is cold. What do you say? _____

_____

3. The customer says the bill is not right. What do you say? _____

_____

Complete the activities below. Write your answers on other paper.

1. Visit a restaurant and ask for a menu to read. Answer the questions below.
   - Does the menu show specials for the day? Does it show a soup of the day?
   - Does the restaurant have appetizers? If so, which appetizers does it have?
   - What desserts does the restaurant have?
   - Does the restaurant serve complete meals? If so, what do the meals come with?

2. With a partner, compare two restaurants that you both know. Discuss these questions:
   - Which restaurant gives better service? Why do you think so?
   - Are the workers who serve food at each restaurant called "servers"?

     Or are they called "waiters" and "waitresses," as in the past?

     Do you prefer "servers" or "waiters" and "waitresses"? Why?
   - Do you tip the servers at these restaurants? If so, when do you leave a big tip? When do you leave a small tip or no tip?
   - Customers leave a tip when they are happy with the server. The tip is usually between ten percent and twenty percent of the bill. Do you think customers should tip servers? Why?

Notes

_____

_____

_____

_____

_____

Unit 4
THE CUSTOMER COMES FIRST!

What is the man doing? What do good servers do before customers arrive?

Words to Know:

bowl	(to) be right	first	it's
dinner	(to) fill	fresh	there's
glass	(to) fold	lucky	they're
job	(to) help	nervous	we're
pitcher	(to) make a mistake		
rhyme	(to) remember	left	Don't worry.
saucer	(to) set the table	right	I get it!
shakers	(to) set up	soon	No problem.
silverware	(to) show		
station	(to) twist		
team			
wineglass			

Listen and Speak

Step 1: Listen as your teacher reads the dialogue.

Elena: Excuse me. It's my first day here. I have to check my station. What do I do?

Bob: The customers will be here soon. You need to set up the tables in your station. Do they have plates, cups, saucers, and silverware?

Elena: Yes. I set all the tables.

Bob: Did you put the napkins in the wineglasses?

Elena: No. I put them on the tables.

Bob: I'll show you how we fold napkins at Las Flores. Twist them like this. It's easy.

Elena: I get it!

Bob: Did you fill the salt, pepper, and sugar shakers?

Elena: Yes. I checked all the tables in my station. They're all full.

Bob: Good. Are there fresh flowers on each table?

Elena: Yes. I checked.

Bob: This table isn't set right. The salad fork goes on the left.

Elena: Oh. I made a mistake!

Bob: No problem. It's easy to fix. Here, I'll help you. We're a team here.

Elena: Thank you for your help. I'm a little nervous.

Bob: Don't worry. Just remember that the customer comes first. Remember the Las Flores rhyme.

Elena: What's that?

Bob: "Always smile and be polite because the customer is always right."

Elena: You're a good worker! Las Flores is lucky. Thank you for your help.

Bob: Thank *you!* I want the customers to come back. I want us *both* to have jobs here.

Step 2: Practice the dialogue with a partner.

Step 3: Talk about the Las Flores rhyme, "Always smile and be polite because the customer is always right." Discuss these questions:
- What is a rhyme?
- Why is the customer always right?

Step 4: Elena says, "I have to check my station." What does that mean? Discuss your answer with your partner.

Practice

Step 1:   Draw a line from the question to the answer.

1. Is this your first day?

2. Did you put napkins in the wineglasses?

3. Do you remember the Las Flores rhyme?

4. Did you fill the salt, pepper, and sugar shakers?

5. Do the tables in your station have plates, cups, saucers, and silverware?

a. "Always smile and be polite because the customer is always right."

b. Yes, it is.

c. Yes. I set all the tables.

d. Yes. They're all full.

e. No, I put them on the tables.

Step 2:   Help a new worker at Las Flores Restaurant. Write on the lines below. Then read the conversation with a partner.

New Worker: This is my first day here. I have to check my station. What do I do?

You: _____

_____?

New Worker: Yes. I set all the tables.

You: _____

New Worker: Oh. I made a mistake! I'm a little nervous.

You: _____.

Just remember that the customer comes first. Remember the Las

Flores rhyme.

New Worker: What's that?

You: _____.

Build Your Vocabulary

Step 1:   Look at the picture. It shows the correct way to set a table.

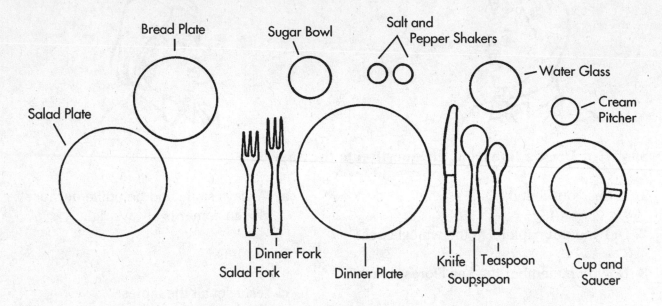

Words to Know:

above below	between in the center (of)	next to on the left (of)	on the right (of) on top (of) under

Step 2:   Circle the word in parentheses that best completes each sentence.

1. The salad fork goes (on the left of, on top of) the dinner fork.

2. The dinner plate goes (above, between) the forks and the knife.

3. The water glass goes (next to, above) the spoons.

4. The knife goes (on the right of, in the center of) the dinner plate.

5. The dinner fork goes (next to, on the right of) the dinner plate.

6. The salad plate goes (under, on the left of) the dinner plate.

7. The soupspoon goes (below, in the center of) the water glass.

8. The cup goes (next to, on top of) the saucer.

9. The salt and pepper shakers go (in the center of, under) the table.

10. The bread plate goes (below, above) the salad fork.

11. The sugar bowl goes (between, in the center of) the table.

12. The saucer goes (above, under) the cup.

salad fork	dinner fork	cup and saucer	water glass
wineglass	teaspoon	dinner plate	soupspoon
cream pitcher	sugar bowl	bread plate	napkin
steak knife	salad plate	knife	salt and pepper shakers

Write the correct word from the box under the picture.

1. _____ 2. _____ 3. _____ 4. _____

5. _____ 6. _____ 7. _____ 8. _____

9. _____ 10. _____ 11. _____ 12. _____

13. _____ 14. _____ 15. _____ 16. _____

Listen and Speak

Words to Know:

attitude	besides
idea	someday
manager	
movie	can't
sir	let's
the movies	
(to) keep	
paid	

Keep the Customer Satisfied

Step 1: Listen as your teacher reads the conversation.

Elena: Are you going to the movies tonight?

Lee: Yes, I am.

Elena: What movie are you going to see?

Lee: *The Big Kiss.*

Customer: Excuse me! I'm ready to order. I can't wait!

Lee: Oh, I'm sorry, sir. May I take your order?

LATER

Elena: Let's wait for our break to talk about movies, OK?

Lee: That's a good idea. I want to keep my job, and I want to be a manager someday. Besides, we're paid to serve customers.

Elena: Right! That's a good attitude. We're not paid to talk about the movies.

Step 2: Read the conversation with a partner.

Step 3: Discuss these questions:
• Why did Elena and Lee stop talking?
• Are Elena and Lee good workers? Why or why not?

Step 1: Use the words from the box to complete the sentences. Use each word or phrase only once. If the word or phrase begins a sentence, use a capital letter.

excuse me	paid
we're	break
wait	I'm sorry
attitude	

1. _____! I'm ready to order. I can't _____.

2. Oh, _____, ma'am. May I take your order?

3. _____ paid to serve customers.

4. We're not _____ to talk about the movies.

5. Let's wait for our _____ to talk about movies, OK?

6. Right! That's a good _____.

Step 2: Circle *True* or *False* for each sentence.

1. A good worker helps customers right away.   True   False

2. It's important to have a good attitude at work.   True   False

3. A worker is only paid to take breaks.   True   False

4. A worker must be polite to all customers.   True   False

5. It's a good idea to tell customers, "Thank you for waiting. I'll be with you in a minute."   True   False

6. A worker must never bring customers what they need.   True   False

7. A worker must not talk about the movies or other personal matters when working.   True   False

8. A worker must not smile at the customers.   True   False

9. A worker must never say, "Thank you."   True   False

10. A worker must be polite even if the customer is not.   True   False

Be a Good Worker

Good servers are polite.
They want to help customers.
Lee is a good server. Read
some of the things she says
to her customers.

"I'll check on your order right now."

"I like my job. I like the customers,
and they like me, too."

"Thank you. Come again soon."

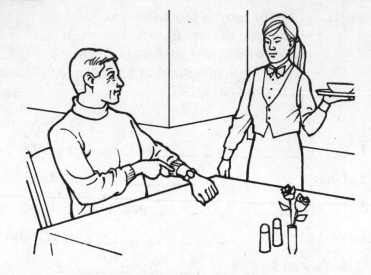

"I'm sorry you had to wait.
We're very busy tonight."

Is This a Good Attitude?

Put a check mark next to the sentences that show a good attitude for a worker.

1. _____ Jamal always smiles at his customers.

2. _____ Diana says "Thank you" to her customers.

3. _____ Sarah talks to another worker when she has customers.

4. _____ Henry doesn't remember his customers' orders.

5. _____ Alicia puts fresh flowers on the tables in her station.

6. _____ Tony tells his customers about the specials.

7. _____ Linda never folds napkins.

8. _____ Sometimes Lupita makes a mistake with her orders. She fixes the mistake, and she tells her customers, "I'm sorry."

9. _____ If a customer has to wait, Marcos apologizes.

10. _____ Sometimes a customer has a problem with the bill. Jean-Louis checks the bill for his customers. If the bill has a mistake, Jean-Louis fixes it.

Use the words in the box to fill in the spaces in the puzzle.

attitude	manager	ready
break	me	team
customer	order	
job	polite	

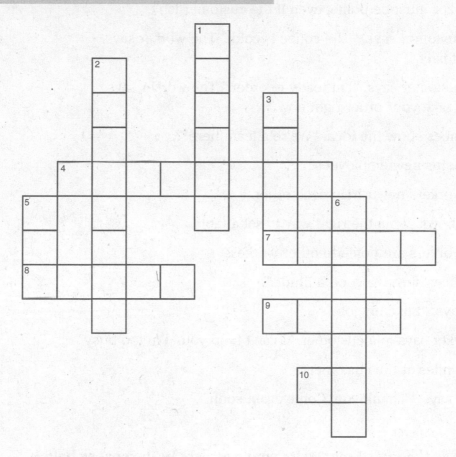

Across

4. Bob has a good _____ about his job.

7. Are you _____ to order?

8. Elena and Lee wait for the _____ to talk.

9. I'll help you. We're a _____ here.

10. Excuse _____.

Down

1. Always smile and be _____

2. The _____ comes first.

3. May I take your _____?

5. I want to keep my _____.

6. The _____ is the boss.

Think It Over

Step 1: Read each question. Put a check mark in the boxes beside the correct answers.

1. Which sentences show the idea, "The customer comes first"?

   ❑ **a.** A worker's job is to bring customers what they need.

   ❑ **b.** A worker must be polite, even if the customer isn't.

   ❑ **c.** The customer says, "The coffee is cold." The worker says, "No, it isn't."

   ❑ **d.** The customer says, "I'm ready to order." The worker says, "I can take your order right now."

2. Which sentences show the idea, "We're a team here"?

   ❑ **a.** Bob helps new employees.

   ❑ **b.** The workers never help each other.

   ❑ **c.** Bob shows Elena the right way to set a table.

   ❑ **d.** The workers are polite to other workers.

3. Which sentences show "a good attitude"?

   ❑ **a.** Lee says, "I like my job."

   ❑ **b.** A worker says to a customer, "I can't help you. I'm too busy."

   ❑ **c.** Bob smiles at the customers.

   ❑ **d.** Elena says, "Thank you. Come again soon."

Step 2: Answer the questions. Write your answers in the spaces below.

1. What does the saying "The customer comes first" mean to you?

   _____

   _____

2. What does "We're a team here" mean to you?

   _____

   _____

3. What does "a good attitude" mean to you?

   _____

   _____

Check Your Understanding

You are a server. Circle the letter of the correct answer.

1. The customer says, "I'm ready to order."

   a. I bring the customer hot coffee.

   b. I say, "I have to go on break."

   c. I say, "May I take your order?"

2. The customer says, "I need a napkin."

   a. I bring the customer hot coffee.

   b. I say, "I'll get one right away."

   c. I say, "I'm too busy."

3. The customer says, "I'm in a hurry. I want my dinner now."

   a. I bring the customer hot coffee.

   b. I set the table.

   c. I say, "OK, I'll check on your order right away."

4. The customer says, "May I have a little coffee, please?"

   a. I bring the customer hot coffee.

   b. I say, "I'm sorry. I'm on my break."

   c. I say, "Are you going to the movies tonight?"

5. The customer says, "I'm ready to order. I can't wait."

   a. I say, "I'll be right with you."

   b. I say, "I'll get you some."

   c. I bring the customer hot coffee.

Complete the activities below. Write your answers on other paper.

1. At home, practice setting a table the way servers do in a restaurant. Ask a relative or a friend to check your work.

2. In a small group, talk about good and bad employee attitudes. Then write three examples of good employee attitudes.

   _____

   _____

   _____

3. Go to a restaurant, or remember the last time you went to a restaurant. Answer the questions below.
   • Did the employees smile, and were they polite?
   • Did the employees work as a team?
   • Did the workers help the customers right away?
   • Did the employees talk about personal matters when working?
   • Did the workers make the customers feel important?
   • Do the customers want to come back to this restaurant? Why or why not?

4. Talk to a partner about a restaurant. Answer the questions from activity 3.

Notes

_____

_____

_____

_____

_____

Unit 5
DO YOU HAVE A RESERVATION?

What "Words to Know" do you see pictured above?
Who are the workers in the picture? What are their jobs?

Words to Know:

booster chair	reservation	probably
bus girl	seat	
bus person		first available
busboy	(to) reserve	right here
capital (letter)	(to) spell	right this way
high chair		right with you
host	available	How long is
hostess	nonsmoking	the wait?
party	smoking	
patio		

Listen and Speak

Step 1: Listen as your teacher reads the dialogue.

Hostess: Good afternoon. Do you have a reservation?

Customer: No, we don't. How long is the wait?

Hostess: Probably twenty or twenty-five minutes.

Customer: OK.

Hostess: May I have your name and will you spell it, please?

Customer: Chen. *C* as in *cat, h–e–n.*

Hostess: How many are there in your party?

Customer: Four, two adults and two children. We need a high chair and a booster chair.

Hostess: Fine. Smoking, nonsmoking, or first available?

Customer: Nonsmoking.

Hostess: Would you like to wait inside or outside?

Customer: We'll take a seat outside on the patio. May we have a menu to read?

Hostess: Certainly. Here you are. We'll call you when your table is ready.

Customer: Thank you.

Hostess: You're welcome.

LATER

Host: Chen, party of four.

Customer: We're right here.

Host: I'll show you to your table. Right this way, please. The busboy is bringing your high chair and booster chair.

Customer: Can we have that table by the window?

Host: Oh, I'm sorry. That table is reserved, but here's a nice table for four.

Customer: That's fine.

Host: Your server will be right with you. Here are your menus. Enjoy your meal.

Step 2: Read the dialogue with a partner.

Step 3: Discuss these questions with a partner.
- **How long is the wait for a table?**
- **What kind of table does the customer want?**
- **What else does the customer need at the table? Why?**

Practice

Put these sentences in order from 1 to 5.

_____ The hostess says, "Good evening. Do you have a reservation?"

_____ The hostess says, "Only about five minutes. What is your name, please?"

_____ The customer says, "Montana, *M* as in *Mary, o–n–t–a–n–a.*"

_____ The hostess says, "Please have a seat, and I'll call you when your table is ready."

_____ The customer says, "No, I don't have a reservation. How long is the wait for two?"

How Do You Spell That?

Step 1:   **Practice these short conversations with a partner.**

Hostess: What's the name, please?

Customer: DiMarco.

Hostess: Is that *D* as in *dog* or *B* as in *boy*?

Customer: *D* as in *dog, i,* capital *M, a–r–c–o.*

Hostess: Thank you.

Hostess: What's your name, please?

Customer: Nguyen.

Hostess: How do you spell that?

Customer: *N* as in *navy, g* as in *George, u–y–e–n.*

Hostess: Thank you.

Step 2:   **Write your information. Read it with a partner.**

You: My name is _____

Host: How do you spell that?

You: _____

_____

Build Your Vocabulary

Step 1: Read the words in the box. Underline any words you don't know.

Words to Know:

everything	(to) look nice	comfortable
	(to) run smoothly	friendly
(to) greet	(to) seat	
(to) hand		well-groomed

Step 2: Now read the story and the dialogues with a partner.

Lena is a hostess and Jay is a host. They greet their customers with smiles. They always look nice and are well-groomed. Lena and Jay must be friendly because they are the first people in the restaurant that the customers meet.

Lena: Yes, we take reservations.

Jay: The wait will be only one or two minutes.

Jay and Lena answer questions and give information to the customers. They also take reservations. They seat the customers and hand them menus.

Lena: Will you need a high chair or a booster chair?

Jay: May I hang up your coat?

Lena and Jay like helping the customers. They like to make them feel comfortable. They give special attention to customers who need extra help. They work with other employees, especially the bus people and servers, so everything runs smoothly. Sometimes they help the busboy to prepare a table or help a server to serve coffee.

Step 3: Discuss these questions.
- Why must Jay and Lena look nice and be well-groomed?
- Why must Jay and Lena be friendly to customers?
- Why do they help other employees?

Step 1: Put a check mark in front of the words that tell about the host and hostess at work.

The host and hostess

___ often help bus people to prepare tables.   ___ greet customers.

___ are never well-groomed.   ___ never look nice.

___ don't answer questions from customers.   ___ give information to customers.

___ hand menus to customers.   ___ seat customers.

___ like helping customers.   ___ take reservations.

___ don't make customers feel comfortable.   ___ work with other employees.

___ give special attention to customers who need it.   ___ help make everything run smoothly.

Step 2: You are a host or hostess. Fill in the spaces with the correct words. Then practice the conversation with a partner:

Host: Good evening. Do you have a _____?

Customer: No. How long is the _____?

Host: Probably ten or fifteen _____.

Customer: OK.

Host: May I have your _____, please?

Customer: Pobel.

Host: How do you _____ that?

Customer: _____.

Host: _____, nonsmoking, or first available?

Customer: _____.

Host: OK. We'll _____ you when your _____ is _____.

Customer: Thank you.

Listen and Speak

Step 1:   Listen as your teacher reads the dialogue.

Step 2:   Read the words in the box.

Step 3:   Read the conversation with a partner.

Words to Know:

basket	clear
brunch	sure
(to) book	completely
(to) bus	
	wheelchair access

Lena: Good evening, City Place Restaurant. This is Lena. How may I help you?

Caller: Do you take reservations?

Lena: Yes, we do.

Caller: I'd like to reserve a table for four people for 7 P.M.

Lena: I'm very sorry. We're completely booked until eight o'clock tonight.

Caller: OK, 8 P.M. will be fine.

Lena: May I have your name, please?

Caller: VanArsdell.

Lena: Will you please spell that?

Caller: *V* as in *victory, a–n,* capital *A, r–s–d–e,* double *l.*

Lena: So that's four for eight o'clock for VanArsdell.

Caller: Yes. Thank you.

Lena: You're welcome. We'll see you at eight.

Caller: Good-bye.

Lena hangs up the phone and calls the busboy, Sam.

Lena: Sam, it's busy tonight. We have to hurry.

Sam: Sure. What do we need?

Lena: Please bus and set up table eleven for a party of six. Also clear table four and check that there are baskets of our fresh bread on all the tables.

Sam: Sure. No problem.

Lena: Thanks a lot.

Step 1: Circle *C* if the customer asks it. Circle *H* if the host or hostess asks it.

1. "Do you have a reservation?"   **C**   **H**

2. "How long is the wait?"   **C**   **H**

3. "How many are there in your party?"   **C**   **H**

4. "Do you take reservations?"   **C**   **H**

5. "How do you spell your name?"   **C**   **H**

Step 2: You are the host or hostess answering the telephone. Take reservations. Fill in the information in the reservation book below.

You: _____?

Caller 1: Yes, I'd like to make reservations for two for 1:30 on Monday.

Caller 2: Yes, I'd like to reserve a table for ten for an office party on Tuesday at noon.

Caller 3: Yes. I'd like a table for four for 12:30 on Monday.

You: _____?

Caller 1: Mollie. *M* as in *Mary,* o, double *l, i–e.*

Caller 2: Glick Company. *G* as in *George, l–i–c–k.*

Caller 3: Hassam. *H* as in *house, a–s–s–a–m.*

You: _____?

Caller: Thank you, too. See you then.

ℛESERVATIONS

| | Monday | | | | | Tuesday | | | |
Name	Number in Party	Time	Table	Comments	Name	Number in Party	Time	Table	Comments
Potter	4	1:00	#8	birthday					

Be a Good Worker

Match the written times with the clocks that show the same time.
Then with a partner, practice saying the times in different ways.

1. It's six fifteen.
   It's a quarter past six.
   It's fifteen after six.

   a. 8:45

2. It's seven thirty.
   It's half past seven.

   b. 12:00

3. It's eight forty-five.
   It's a quarter to nine.
   It's fifteen minutes to nine.
   It's fifteen minutes before nine.

   c. 2:00

4. It's 12:00 P.M.
   It's noon.
   It's 12:00 A.M.
   It's midnight.

   d. 7:25

5. It's seven twenty-five.
   It's twenty-five after seven.

   e. 7:30

6. It's two o'clock.
   It's two o'clock sharp.

   f. 6:15

Early, On Time, or Late?

It's important for workers to be early or on time for work. Read each item.
Write *early*, *on time*, or *late* to complete each sentence correctly.

1. Jay starts work today at half past four.
   He arrives at this time:

   He is _____.

2. Sam begins work at 6:00 A.M.
   He arrives at this time:

   He arrives _____.

3. Another busboy arrives at this time to
   begin work at seven o'clock:

   He arrives _____.

4. Lena can go home at nine forty-five
   tonight. She leaves at this time:

   She leaves _____.

Have Some Fun!

available	party	host
booster	spell	hostess
restaurant	enjoy	welcome
reservation	meal	high chair

The twelve words in the box are scrambled below. Unscramble them.
Then write the unscrambled words on the lines.

1. ratpy _____

2. iesrervtano _____

3. lame _____

4. lepsl _____

5. mewceol _____

6. ttnuraraes _____

7. orebsto _____

8. lelviabaa _____

9. yejon _____

10. rihihchag _____

11. shsetso _____

12. tohs _____

Find-A-Word Puzzle

Find all of the words from the box in the puzzle below. The words may be horizontal, vertical, or diagonal. They may even be backwards! Circle the words you find.

R	E	S	E	R	V	A	T	I	O	N
I	E	N	J	O	Y	S	H	S	Y	E
U	W	S	G	O	S	R	I	P	T	L
C	E	R	T	E	M	O	G	E	R	B
A	L	R	T	A	E	Y	H	L	A	A
N	C	S	I	M	U	M	C	L	P	L
B	O	O	S	T	E	R	H	G	Y	I
H	M	E	H	A	R	H	A	O	O	A
S	E	E	L	Y	E	S	I	N	U	V
T	R	Y	T	S	O	H	R	E	T	A

Think It Over

Step 1: You are the host or hostess at City Place Restaurant.
Match the telephone questions with your answers.
Write the letter of the correct answer on each line.

Questions

1. _____ "Are you open on Sunday?"

2. _____ "Where is the restaurant?"

3. _____ "What time do you serve dinner?"

4. _____ "Are children welcome?"

5. _____ "How long is the wait for two if we come over right now?"

6. _____ "Do you have wheelchair access?"

7. _____ "Can I make reservations for brunch for this weekend?"

8. _____ "Do you have high chairs and booster chairs for our children?"

Answers

a. "Certainly. We have full wheelchair access."

b. "Sorry, but we only serve brunch in the summer."

c. "We're on the corner of Beech and Fourth."

d. "Yes. This is a family restaurant."

e. "Yes, we're open on Sundays, 9:00 to 9:00."

f. "Yes, we have special chairs for children and coloring books, too."

g. "There's no waiting for a table at this time."

h. "We serve dinner between 5:00 P.M. and 10:00 P.M."

Step 2: Under each clock, write the letters of the sentences that tell the correct time. There is more than one answer for each clock.

1. `12:15`

_____

2. `5:30`

_____

3. `7:45`

_____

a. It's a quarter to eight.

b. It's five thirty.

c. It's seven forty-five.

d. It's a quarter past twelve.

e. It's twelve fifteen.

f. It's half past five.

4. (clock)

_____

5. `7:05`

_____

6. (clock)

_____

a. It's five to twelve.

b. It's seven–o–five.

c. It's five past seven.

d. It's five after seven.

e. It's six twenty-five.

f. It's eleven fifty-five.

g. It's twenty-five after six.

Check Your Understanding

Choose the best answer for a host or hostess.

1. A caller says, "I want to book a table." What do you say?

   a. "I can show you to a table."

   b. "How may I help you?"

   c. "When would you like the reservation for?"

2. A caller wants to make a reservation for Friday night at 6:30 P.M., but you're completely booked for that time. What do you say?

   a. "I'm sorry, but we're completely booked until 7:30 on Friday."

   b. "When would you like the reservation for?"

   c. "May I have your name, please?"

3. You want the bus girl to set up a table for a party of eight. What do you say?

   a. "How many are there in your party?"

   b. "Please set up table six for a party of eight right away."

   c. "Is this eight people for a birthday party?"

4. You don't hear clearly what the phone caller is saying. What do you say?

   a. "Do you have a reservation?"

   b. "How may I help you?"

   c. "Could you please speak a little louder? I can't hear you."

Write an answer to these questions. Then act out each situation with a partner.

1. A customer has small children with him. What do you say? _____
   _____

2. After you seat the customers and give them menus, what do you say? _____
   _____
   _____

Complete three of the activities below.

1. Pretend you are a host or hostess and your partner is a customer. Take four reservations from your partner and write them in your book. Then change roles and make up reservations for your partner to write in the book.

RESERVATIONS

Name	Number in Party	Time	Table	Comments	Name	Number in Party	Time	Table	Comments
Potter	4	1:00	#8	birthday					

2. Work with three other students. Ask the questions below and write (letter by letter) what your partners tell you.

What is your first name? How do you spell it?

1. _____ 2. _____ 3. _____

What is your last name? How do you spell it?

1. _____ 2. _____ 3. _____

3. With a partner, practice spelling people's names. Take turns writing down the letters your partner says. You can use the names of your relatives, classmates, or teachers. You can also use the names from a telephone book.

4. Call a local restaurant. Ask if they take reservations. If you would like to eat there, make a reservation.

Notes

_____

_____

_____

_____

_____

Unit 6
TAKE YOUR TRAY AND COME THIS WAY

Look at the picture. The workers are standing in a serving line. What do you think a serving line is? What other words from the box below do you see in the picture?

Words to Know:

booth	split pea soup	low
cafeteria	trainee	major
cashier	vegetarian	patient
chicken noodle	vegetable soup	
soup	weekdays	mine
crackers		
cream of	(to) be sure	à la carte
mushroom soup	(to) carry	in other words
entree	(to) decide	two for one
navy bean soup	(to) find out	
potato cheese soup	(to) follow	
serving line	(to) sound good	
soup du jour		

Listen and Speak

Step 1: Listen as your teacher reads the conversation.

Server A: Hi! Welcome to the Country Cafeteria.

Customer: Hi. Do you have any specials?

Server A: Yes. We have our early bird special from 4:00 to 6:00 P.M. weekdays.

Customer: That sounds good. What is it?

Server A: You get one entree, a salad, two side dishes, and a beverage for one low price. Or you can buy items à la carte.

Customer: OK. Oh, what is your soup du jour?

Server A: Let's check the menu on the wall. Our soup today is vegetarian vegetable.

Customer: I'll take a bowl, please.

Server A: Here you are. Would you like some crackers?

Customer: Yes, please. Can my husband and I use this two-for-one coupon?

Server A: I'm not sure. Let me find out for you.

Server B
(to customer): You can use the coupon. Just show it to the cashier. Enjoy your meal.

Server A
(to Server B): Thanks. I'm a trainee. This is my first time on the serving line.

Server B: You'll do fine. Just be friendly and patient. The customers need time to decide. Oh, and be sure to make eye contact and smile.

LATER

Cashier: That will be $12.97.

Customer: Do you take credit cards?

Cashier: Yes, we do. We take all major cards.

LATER

Server C: May I carry your tray for you? And would you like a table or a booth?

Customer: No, thanks, I can carry my tray. And we would like a table.

Server C: Certainly. Please take your trays and come this way.

Step 2: Write two questions about the conversation. The questions should be about words or ideas that you don't understand.

Step 3: Form a group of five students. Read the conversation in your group.

Step 4: Look at the questions you wrote. Discuss them with your group.

Step 1:   Look at the menu. Then check Yes or No
           to answer the questions below.

1. Today is Monday. Can Marie order
   chicken noodle soup?

   _____ Yes   _____ No

2. Jessica wants split pea soup.
   Can she order it on Tuesday?

   _____ Yes   _____ No

3. Tom wants potato cheese soup.
   Can he order it on Wednesday?

   _____ Yes   _____ No

Step 2:   Read each question. Then write your answer in the space
           after each question.

4. What soup can Philip get on Thursday? _____

5. What soup can Alicia get on Sunday? _____

6. David likes clam chowder and French onion soup. On what days can he get those soups?

   _____

What's the Answer?

Draw a line from the question to the correct answer.

Question

1. What's the soup today?

2. Can we use this coupon?

3. Do you have an early bird special?

4. What is the early bird special?

5. May we have a booth?

6. Do you take credit cards?

Answer

a. Soup or salad is included free with
   your entree.

b. Sure. Here's a booth for you.

c. Yes, you can use the coupon.

d. Yes. We take all major cards.

e. Yes, we do, until 5:30.

f. Let me find out for you. I think it's
   French onion.

Build Your Vocabulary

Step 1: Read what the manager of Country Cafeteria says below. The manager is speaking to new workers.

Words to Know:

appearance	thermometer	(to) change
cold table		(to) let
edge	bottom	(somebody)
eye appeal	higher	know
look	hottest	(to) make sure
pan	proud	(to) pour
patrons		(to) run out of
portion	(to) burn	(to) stay even
steam table	(to) buy	(to) stir
temperature	(to) calibrate	(to) succeed

Welcome to our new employees. We are happy to have you as trainees at the Country Cafeteria. You'll be working on the serving line. That means you'll be working by the steam tables and the cold tables. Be careful not to burn yourselves on the steam tables.

We're very proud of the appearance of our restaurant. We have a lot of repeat patrons, so we have to change our look every day. We want our restaurant, our serving line, and our food to have eye appeal. Remember, we want our patrons to buy our food. As we always say here, "Eye appeal is buy appeal." In other words, if it appeals to the eye, the customer will buy it.

We also want you to succeed. Here are some important things to remember when you work on the serving line:

- This is a food thermometer. Every morning, put it in ice water to calibrate it.
- We use it to check the temperature of the hot food every thirty minutes.
- Stir the food in the pans often so the temperature will stay even.
- Use a clean serving spoon for each new pan.
- Serve from the bottom of the pan, where the food is the hottest.

- Make sure that the portion you serve doesn't go over the edge of the plate.
- Never pour food from a fresh pan into a pan on the steam table.
- Let the kitchen know when a serving pan is running out of food.
- To keep the food at the correct temperature, make sure that the food in the serving pan is not higher than the edge of the pan.

Step 2: Work with a partner. Look at the words in the box. Find those words in the reading and underline them. How is each word used? How does the reading help you understand what the words mean?

Place a check mark next to each sentence that is correct.

_____ 1. A trainee is a new employee.

_____ 2. The steam tables are cold.

_____ 3. You can burn yourself on the steam tables.

_____ 4. Serve food from the top of the pan.

_____ 5. Check the temperature of the hot food every two hours.

_____ 6. Stir the food in the pans so the temperature will stay even.

_____ 7. Put the food thermometer in ice water to calibrate it.

_____ 8. Use a thermometer to check the temperature of the hot food.

_____ 9. The food should always be higher than the edge of the pan.

_____ 10. Use a clean serving spoon for each new pan.

_____ 11. Make sure the portion you serve fits the plate.

_____ 12. Never pour food from a fresh pan into a pan on the steam table.

_____ 13. Let the kitchen know when a serving pan is running out of food.

_____ 14. The food in a restaurant should have eye appeal.

_____ 15. The manager says, "Eye appeal is buy appeal."

Listen and Speak

Step 1: Listen as your teacher reads the conversation.

Words to Know:

condiment		appetizing
containers	(to) add	crushed
matches	(to) finish	greasy
mayo	(to) refill	sticky
mints	(to) replace	wonderful
packets	(to) separate	
side work	(to) wipe	lots
sneeze guard		
toothpicks		

Karl: Can I do anything to help? I finished my side work.

Linda: Thank you for asking. Could you please clean up and refill the salad bar?

Karl: How do I do that?

Linda: You have to clean the sneeze guard and wipe around each of the containers. Then bring out more food to refill the containers. Oh, and see if you need to add more ice.

LATER

Linda: Now the food looks appetizing.

Karl: Thanks. Do you need some more help?

Linda: Sure. You can check the baskets on the condiment stand. Make sure there are lots of packets of sugar. And separate the mustard, mayo, ketchup, and relish packets. Also replace any crushed crackers.

LATER

Linda: The condiment stand looks great, Karl. It's nice and neat.

Karl: Thanks. I'd be happy to help some more.

Linda: Wonderful! You can make sure all of the salt and pepper shakers are filled, and the outsides are cleaned off. They get greasy and sticky.

Karl: I'll do it right now.

Linda: Thanks. And if you want something else to do, the baskets near the cashier need refilling with mints, toothpicks, and matches.

Karl: No problem!

Linda: We'll have no problem getting the side work done!

Step 2: Find a partner. Read the conversation together out loud.

Step 3: Make a list of side work that Linda asks Karl to do.

Step 4: Discuss the following questions:
- What is side work?
- Is side work important? Why?

Practice

Circle *True* or *False* for each sentence.

1.	Karl already knows how to clean and refill the salad bar.	True	False
2.	Karl cleans the sneeze guard.	True	False
3.	Linda says the food looks appetizing.	True	False
4.	Linda asks Karl to help the customers.	True	False
5.	Karl offers to help Linda with the side work.	True	False
6.	Linda tells Karl, "Thank you for asking."	True	False
7.	Karl separates the condiment packets.	True	False
8.	Karl likes to help.	True	False
9.	Linda likes Karl to help her.	True	False
10.	Linda likes Karl's work.	True	False

Time for Side Work!

Choose a word from the box to complete each sentence below.

Add	Refill
Check	Replace
Clean	Separate
Make sure	

1. _____ the salad bar containers with more food.

2. _____ the sneeze guard on the salad bar.

3. _____ more ice to the salad bar.

4. _____ the condiment stand to make sure there are lots of packets.

5. _____ crushed crackers.

6. _____ the mustard, mayo, ketchup, and relish packets.

7. _____ all of the salt and pepper shakers are filled.

Be a Good Worker

A good worker offers to help other workers. A good worker also asks the supervisor if anything special needs to be done. Place a check mark next to the things that show what a good worker says.

_____ 1. "Can I do anything to help?"

_____ 2. "I'd be happy to help some more."

_____ 3. "I don't want to help."

_____ 4. "Is there anything special that I can do before I leave?"

_____ 5. "You can do it yourself."

_____ 6. "I'm too tired to help right now."

_____ 7. "Can you do it by yourself, or do you need my help?"

_____ 8. "What can I do to help?"

_____ 9. "I'm going home."

A good worker keeps the cafeteria clean and refills the food and condiments. Circle the letters of the answers that show a good worker. More than one answer may be correct.

10. A worker helps a restaurant have eye appeal when he or she
    a. keeps the condiment stand neat.
    b. keeps pans full.
    c. leaves salt and pepper shakers empty.
    d. keeps the restaurant clean.

11. The salad bar looks appetizing when the worker
    a. cleans the sneeze guard.
    b. wipes around each of the containers and fills them with food.
    c. doesn't refill the salad bar.
    d. adds more ice.

12. A serving line worker doesn't do a good job when he or she
    a. serves food from the bottom of the pan.
    b. uses the same spoon for all pans.
    c. checks the temperature of hot foods every thirty minutes.
    d. forgets to stir the food in the pan.

Have Some Fun!

Use the clues below and the words in the box to complete the crossword puzzle.

appearance	condiments
booth	pan
calibrate	thermometer
cashier	trainee

Across

1. Please pay the _____.

4. Mustard, ketchup, and relish are _____.

7. Put the thermometer in ice water to _____ it.

8. The new worker is a _____.

Down

2. The _____ of the serving line is important.

3. Would you like a table or a _____?

5. Check the temperature of the food with a _____.

6. Use a spoon to stir the food in the _____.

Think It Over

Most workers in food service do side work. Servers do side work when they aren't helping customers and before they leave for the day. Side work helps a cafeteria or restaurant look good and be ready for customers. Circle the pictures below that show side work. Under each picture, write a sentence to tell a worker how to do the side work.

1.

_____

_____

2.

_____

_____

3.

_____

_____

4.

_____

_____

Check Your Understanding

Read each question. Circle the letter of the best answer.

1. Do you take credit cards?

   a. I don't know.

   b. I'm not sure. I'll find out for you.

   c. What do you think?

2. What kind of soup do you have?

   a. I'll take a bowl, please.

   b. Would you like some crackers?

   c. Our soups today are cream of mushroom and navy bean.

3. Would you carry my tray for me?

   a. Take your tray and come this way.

   b. Yes. I'd be happy to do it.

   c. No, thank you.

4. Can I do anything to help?

   a. Wonderful. The condiment stand looks nice and neat.

   b. Yes. Please refill the salad bar.

   c. No!

5. This is my first day. What do I do?

   a. Take your tray and come this way.

   b. We take all major credit cards.

   c. Just be friendly and patient.

6. Do you have any specials?

   a. The customers need time to decide.

   b. Just be patient and friendly.

   c. We have a two-for-one special.

7. Can we use this coupon?

   a. Yes, just show it to the cashier.

   b. I don't know.

   c. You can buy items à la carte.

8. Your special sounds good. What is it?

   a. Here you are.

   b. You can use the coupon.

   c. Soup or salad is free with your entree.

9. Are the steam tables hot?

   a. Yes. Be careful. You can burn yourself on them.

   b. No, they aren't.

   c. Talk to the manager.

10. Can you do it by yourself?

    a. Yes, thanks. I'm OK.

    b. I have to go home.

    c. Do you need help?

**Complete the first two activities in class on another sheet of paper.
Then choose one other activity to do after class.**

1. What does "Eye appeal is buy appeal" mean to you?
   Write your answer in a paragraph.

2. Work with a partner. Pretend you are ordering your favorite entree in a restaurant.
   Discuss these questions:
   • What entree will you order?
   • How do you expect your food to look?
   • How important is the appearance of your food?
   • Why is appearance important?

3. Go to a cafeteria and look at the food. Does the food look appetizing to you?
   Answer yes or no, then give three reasons for your answer.

4. Go to a cafeteria. Ask the workers what side work they do. Write the answers and share
   them with your class.

5. Look through the coupons in the Sunday newspaper. What restaurant coupons
   do you see? Bring them to class and share the coupons with other students.
   Compare the coupons and answer these questions:
   • What do the coupons say?
   • Which coupon is the best offer? Why?
   • Which coupon would you use? Why?

Notes

_____

_____

_____

_____

_____

Unit 7
SAFETY MATTERS

Look at the picture. What words from the box below do you see in the picture? What do you think the workers are talking about?

Words to Know:

accident	metal	(to) pay attention	safety
award	microwave oven	(to) report	slippery
cooking surface	pots	(to) slip	unsafe
electrical	rules	(to) spill	wet
equipment	shift	(to) store	
eye level	sign	(to) think so	immediately
fire	utensils	(to) turn off	
foil	warning	(to) unplug	Me neither.
handle		(to) win	Oh, yeah.
hazard	(to) fall		turned inward
liquids	(to) matter	caution	Watch your step!
meeting	(to) mop	free	

Listen and Speak

Step 1: Listen as your teacher reads the conversation.

Hector: Watch your step! Look at the caution sign. The floor is wet and slippery. That's a safety hazard. I spilled some water, and I have to mop it up.

Tom: Thanks for warning me. I don't want to slip and fall.

Hector: Me neither. I want our shift to be accident free. Then we can win the safety award. We can win five extra minutes on all our breaks all month!

Tom: Oh, yeah. They talked about that at the meeting this morning.

Hector: That's why we're going to make a big sign with kitchen safety rules.

Tom: That's a good idea. As they say, "Safety matters!"

THE NEXT DAY

Hector: The sign is ready. What do you think of it?

Tom: It looks great.

Hector: I think so, too.

Safety Rules

1. Clean up spilled food or water immediately.
2. Put up a caution sign when floor is wet.
3. Be careful with hot liquids, hot utensils, hot cooking surfaces, and hot oil. They can burn you and start fires.
4. Always report unsafe conditions or equipment to the manager.
5. Be careful with knives, and don't leave them underwater.
6. Be sure to keep handles of pots and pans turned inward.
7. Never store liquids above eye level.
8. Unplug electrical equipment before cleaning.
9. Never put foil or metals in a microwave oven.
10. Be careful! Pay attention to what you are doing!

Step 2: Read the conversation with a partner. Then read the safety rules together.

Step 3: Talk about the safety rules. Which rules do you already know? Which rules don't you understand? Why?

Look at the pictures. Match a picture with one of the safety rules below.
Draw a line from the picture to the safety rule.

1.

3.

2.

4.

a. Unplug electrical equipment before
you clean it.

b. Be careful with hot liquids and utensils.

c. Be sure to carry knives carefully.

d. Be sure to keep handles of pots and pans
turned inward.

Write the Rules

Fill in the safety rules with words from the box.
Use each word or phrase once.

foil	caution sign
manager	metals
spilled	knives

1. Clean up _____ food or
   water immediately.

2. Put up a _____ when the floor is wet.

3. Always report unsafe conditions or equipment to the _____.

4. Never put _____ or _____ in a microwave oven.

5. Don't leave _____ underwater.

Build Your Vocabulary

Step 1: Read what the restaurant manager says at a safety meeting for workers.

Words to Know:

blade	dangerous	(to) dry
cloth	falling	(to) place
cutting board	sharp	(to) pry open
pad		(to) wash
slicer		

"Today I'm going to talk about knife safety. Always cut on a cutting board and cut away from your body. *Don't* bring a knife toward you. We keep our knives very sharp so they cut well. That means they are dangerous and can cut you easily.

"I wrote some rules for knife safety on the board. I'm going to leave them on the board for everyone to read."

Safety Rules for Using Knives

1. Never play with knives. A knife is a tool to be used.
2. Do not cut anything until someone shows you how to use the knife.
3. When you carry a knife, always point it toward the floor.
4. Be sure your hands and the knife handle are dry before using or carrying a knife.
5. Never use a knife to pry anything open.
6. Never try to catch a falling knife.
7. Never leave a knife underwater. Clean it and immediately put it away.
8. Don't pass a knife to anyone. Place it in front of the person with the blade pointing away from both of you.
9. The slicer is also sharp and dangerous. Never clean the blade with a cloth. Use a thick pad.

Step 2: Work with a partner. Look at the words in the box. Then read the safety rules. Talk about any words you don't understand.

Step 3: For each rule, discuss how a person might get hurt if someone breaks the rule.

How many safety hazards do you see in the picture?
Write six hazards on the lines under the picture.

1. _____

_____

2. _____

_____

3. _____

_____

4. _____

_____

5. _____

_____

6. _____

_____

Listen and Speak

Words to Know:

911	smoke alarm	(to) squeeze
baking soda	stove	
base		burning
fire	(to) aim	
extinguisher	(to) cover	quickly
flames	(to) grab	
grease	(to) pull	Don't panic!
noise	(to) put out	going out
nozzle	(to) smell	sweeping
pin	(to) smother	motion

Step 1: Listen as your teacher reads the conversation about two restaurant workers and a fire.

Hector: What's that noise?

Tom: It's probably the smoke alarm.

Hector: I smell smoke. Something is burning.

Tom: Oh, no! Flames are coming from the top of the stove.

Hector: Someone spilled some grease and didn't clean it up. Don't panic! We have to move quickly. Tom, grab the fire extinguisher.

Tom: I don't know how to use it.

Hector: I'll show you. First, pull the pin.

Tom: Like this?

Hector: Yes. Now aim the nozzle at the base of the fire.

Tom: OK. Next?

Hector: Squeeze the handle and use a sweeping motion.

Tom: Oh, it's going out.

Hector: Good work! We put out that fire quickly! We didn't need to call 911 this time.

Step 2: Work with a partner. Read the conversation out loud.

Step 3: Discuss these questions with your partner:
- How did the fire start?
- How did the workers put out the fire?
- What is a fire extinguisher? What does it do?
- How do you use a fire extinguisher?
- What is 911?

To use a fire extinguisher, remember the word *pass*.

P = *Pull* the pin.
A = *Aim* the nozzle at the base of the fire.
S = *Squeeze* the handle.
S = Use a *sweeping* motion.

Write the steps in using a fire extinguisher. Then draw a line to the picture that goes with each step.

1. _____

   _____

a.

2. _____

   _____

b.

Pin

3. _____

   _____

c.

Nozzle

4. _____

   _____

d.

Handle

Be a Good Worker

Step 1: Listen as your teacher reads the information about fire.

Fire needs three elements: **air, heat,** and **fuel.** Fuel can be wood, grease, or even clothes. To put out a fire, a good worker takes away one of the three elements. Firefighters use water to put out most fires. But water makes a grease fire or an electrical fire worse! You can pour baking soda on these fires to smother them and put them out.

Step 2: Read the information about fire to yourself. Then discuss these questions with the class.
- How can you put out most fires?
- How can you put out a grease fire or an electrical fire?
- What is baking soda? How does it put out a fire?

Step 3: Look at the sentences below. Which element can you take away to put out a fire or keep it from starting? Write the correct element—air, heat, or fuel— in each space below. The first one is done for you.

1. You work in a kitchen with lots of grease. You wear short or tight sleeves in the kitchen.

   You take away the _____*fuel*_____.

2. A fire starts in a greasy pan. You cover the fire with a lid.

   You take away the _____.

3. The toast in the toaster is on fire. You unplug the toaster.

   You take away the _____.

4. A pan of potatoes is burning on the stove. You turn off the stove.

   You take away the _____.

5. A grease fire starts in a pan. You cover the fire with baking soda.

   You take away the _____.

6. You spill grease on the stove. You quickly clean up the spilled grease.

   You take away the _____.

7. A customer puts his menu too close to a lit candle. The menu starts to smoke.

   You take the menu away.

   You take away the _____.

Have Some Fun!

Read the clues for the crossword puzzle.
Then fill in the puzzle with words from the box.

aim	cover	foil	mop
blade	falling	handle	rules
board	fire	knives	slippery

Across

5. Never try to catch a
_____ knife.

6. Never put _____ in a
microwave oven.

7. Use a _____ to clean up
spilled liquid on the floor.

8. You can put out a grease fire if you
_____ the pan with a lid.

9. Squeeze the _____ of a
fire extinguisher to put out a fire.

11. It's important to follow safety
_____ .

Down

1. It's dangerous to walk on a
_____ floor.

2. Never play with _____ .

3. Always use a cutting _____ .

4. The _____ of a knife is sharp.

5. Use an extinguisher to put out a
_____ .

10. _____ the fire extinguisher
at the base of a fire.

Think It Over

aim	pull	squeeze
cover	put	store
don't panic	report	turn off
fall	slip	use
pry	smell	

Write the correct word or phrase from the box in each sentence below.
Use each word or phrase once. If the word or phrase begins a sentence,
use a capital letter.

1. _____ the pan to put out a grease fire.

2. "I _____ smoke!"

3. _____ the pin.

   _____ the nozzle at the base of the fire.

   _____ the handle.

   _____ a sweeping motion.

4. Don't _____ and _____ on that wet floor.

5. _____ the stove under that smoky pan.

6. _____ unsafe conditions to the manager.

7. Never use a knife to _____ anything open.

8. Never _____ water on a grease or electrical fire!

9. _____ when there's a fire.

10. Never _____ liquids above eye level.

Check Your Understanding

Answer the questions. You can find the answers in this unit.

1. There is a potato peel on the floor. How do you warn your co-worker?

_____

2. There is foil on the plate for the microwave. What do you say about that?

_____

3. Your co-worker puts cooking oil on a shelf over the stove. What do you say?

_____

_____

4. The food slicer is unsafe. What do you say to the manager?

_____

5. Your co-worker is pointing a knife like a bad guy in a movie. What do you say?

_____

6. There is a fire on the stove. What do you say to your co-worker?

_____

7. The floor is wet and there is no caution sign. What do you say?

_____

8. There is a fire in the toaster. What do you say to the worker next to the toaster?

_____

9. You have to show your co-worker how to use the fire extinguisher. What do you say?

_____

_____

10. Your co-worker asks you what the manager talked about at the knife safety meeting. What do you say?

_____

_____

Complete the first activity. Then do two other activities outside of class. Write your answers on other paper.

1. Form a group of four or five students. On a piece of paper, write three possible safety hazards in a restaurant. Also write the way to correct each safety hazard. Don't show your paper to the other students. Take turns reading a hazard. Let the other students think of a way to fix the problem. The first student who gives a correct answer reads the next hazard.

2. Look around your home and your school for safety hazards. You may want to use the safety rules on pages 74 and 76 as a guide. List any hazards you see and find out if someone can fix them. Answer these questions:
   • What is the hazard? How do you know it is a hazard?
   • Who can fix the problem? How?

3. Call or visit a fire station. Find out how to report a fire emergency in your community. Ask these questions:
   • What kinds of fires can I put out myself?
   • When should I call the fire department?
   • What can I do to avoid a kitchen fire?

4. Visit two different restaurants. Ask the managers at each restaurant to name the most important safety rules that workers must follow. Make a list for each set of safety rules. Then compare the two lists. Answer these questions:
   • Which safety rules do both restaurants have?
   • Which safety rules from this lesson are on your lists?
   • Which restaurant do you think is safest for its workers? Why?

Notes

_____

_____

_____

_____

_____

Unit 8
HOT THINGS HOT, COLD THINGS COLD

Read the words in the box. Underline any words you don't know.
Then look at the picture. What are the two workers looking at? Why?

Words to Know:

bacteria		broken
boss	may	maximum
degrees Celsius (°C)	(to) break	minimum
degrees Fahrenheit (°F)	(to) get busy	reach-in
food poisoning	(to) get sick	walk-in
food warmer	(to) grow	
freezer	(to) guess	it reads . . .
germs	(to) spoil	supposed to
reading	(to) stay	Uh-oh!
refrigerator	(to) throw away	What's wrong . . .?
responsibility		

Listen and Speak

Step 1: Listen as your teacher reads the dialogue.

Sally: Something is wrong with the thermometer on this reach-in refrigerator.

Ty: What's wrong with it?

Sally: I think it's broken. Look, it reads eighty-two degrees Fahrenheit.

Ty: Uh-oh! That's not good. It's supposed to read between thirty-five and forty-five degrees. We have to tell the boss.

Sally: I guess so. The food might spoil.

Ty: You're right.

LATER

Sally: The boss was glad that we reported the high reading on the thermometer.

Ty: Was the food OK?

Sally: No, the refrigerator was broken. We have to throw all the food away.

Ty: Oh no! That's too bad.

Sally: Well, the food inside has to stay cold or bacteria will grow.

Ty: Bacteria?

Sally: You know, germs. We don't want anyone to get sick with food poisoning. The customer's safety is our number one responsibility.

Ty: That's for sure! It's lucky it was the reach-in refrigerator and not the walk-in that broke. There's a lot more food in the walk-in. And a lot more for us to clean up.

Sally: You're right. Now let's check the thermometer on the food warmer. What does it read?

Ty: It reads 150 degrees Fahrenheit.

Sally: That's fine. Hot foods need to stay above 140 degrees.

Ty: I'll remember that.

Sally: Yeah, we have to keep hot things hot enough and cold things cold enough.

Ty: OK. Now let's get busy throwing that spoiled food away and cleaning up.

Step 2: Read the dialogue out loud with a partner. Then discuss these questions:
- Why did Sally and Ty report the thermometer reading to their boss?
- What is food poisoning? How do people get food poisoning?
- What is a safe temperature for foods in a refrigerator? In a food warmer?

Step 1: Look at the thermometer. The mark ° means degrees, either in Fahrenheit (F) or Celsius (C). So 150° is the same as 150 degrees. Read the sentences below.

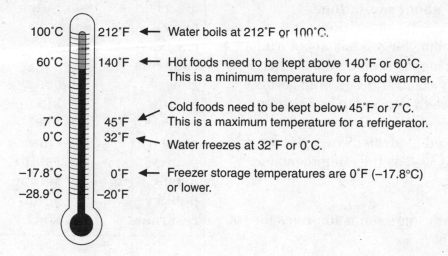

100°C   212°F ← Water boils at 212°F or 100°C.

60°C   140°F ← Hot foods need to be kept above 140°F or 60°C. This is a minimum temperature for a food warmer.

Cold foods need to be kept below 45°F or 7°C. This is a maximum temperature for a refrigerator.

7°C   45°F
0°C   32°F ← Water freezes at 32°F or 0°C.

−17.8°C   0°F ← Freezer storage temperatures are 0°F (−17.8°C) or lower.
−28.9°C   −20°F

Step 2: Draw lines to connect the items on the left with the correct temperatures.

1. Water freezes at   **a.** 140° F, or 60° C.

2. Water boils at   **b.** 32° F, or 0° C.

3. Cold foods need to be kept below   **c.** 0° F or −17.8° C.

4. Hot foods need to be kept above   **d.** 212° F, or 100° C.

5. Freezer storage temperatures are   **e.** 45° F, or 7° C.

Step 3: Write the temperature, in Fahrenheit degrees, under each thermometer. Then mark an X on the temperature that is best for keeping hot foods hot. Circle the temperature that is best for keeping foods cold but not frozen.

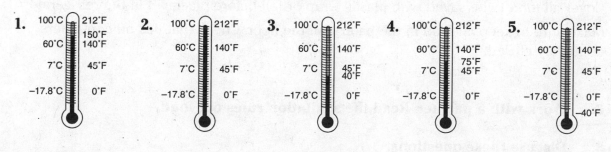

Build Your Vocabulary

Step 1: **Read the information below. A restaurant manager is talking to her employees about sanitation.**

Words to Know:

bandage	room	(to) sterilize
bleach	sanitation	(to) sweep
body	soap	(to) unload
checklist	zone	
elements		harmful
gloves	(to) empty	raw
health	(to) kill	separate
operation	(to) load	sterile
ourselves	(to) rinse	
pantry	(to) sanitize	tightly
plastic wrap	(to) scrape	
poultry	(to) scrub	
rest room	(to) stack	

"Today I'm going to talk about sanitation. Sanitation means keeping the kitchen completely clean and free from germs to prevent health dangers to our customers and ourselves. We have to sanitize raw food, cooked food, all dishes, glasses, and utensils, as well as the equipment and ourselves.

"Here are some sanitation rules for you to remember:

1. Always wash your hands with hot water and soap when you begin your shift, after changing from one operation to another, and after using the rest room.

2. If you have a cut on your hand, put a bandage on it and always wear gloves.

3. Follow the checklist so you can remember to keep the kitchen clean and sanitary.

4. Protect against harmful bacteria in food by checking the thermometers. Bacteria grow quickly between 45° F and 140° F (7° C and 60° C). This is the danger zone for food.

5. Everything that touches food must be sterile, that is, completely free from germs.

6. Keep the cutting boards for meat, fish, and poultry, and non-meat foods separate. Never cut meat on the non-meat cutting board, or non-meat on the meat cutting board.

7. Wash all cutting boards with soap and water first. Then rinse the meat cutting board with a 10 percent bleach solution to kill germs and sterilize it.

8. Cover all food to be saved with plastic wrap or foil before placing it in the refrigerator.

9. Make sure to keep all food in the pantry off the floor. Check that lids on containers are tightly closed."

Step 2: **Work with a partner. Read the sanitation rules out loud.**

Step 3: **Discuss these questions.**
- **Do you follow any of the rules at home? Name any rules you follow.**
- **Which rules are new to you?**
- **Are any of the rules confusing? Talk with your partner about any rules you don't understand.**
- **Why is each rule important? Give one reason for each rule.**

Choose words from the manager's sanitation rules to complete these sentences.

1. Protect against harmful _____ in food by checking the thermometers. Bacteria _____ quickly between 45° and 140° F, and especially at body temperature and room temperature. This is a _____ for food.

2. Make sure to keep all food in the _____ off the floor. Check that lids on containers are _____ closed.

3. Always wash your hands with hot water and _____ when you begin your shift, after changing from one _____ to another, and after using the _____.

4. If you have a cut on your hand, put a _____ on it and always wear _____.

5. Everything that touches _____ must be sterile, that is, completely free from _____.

Check It Out!

Step 1: Read each sentence below. Put a check mark in the box if the sentence shows what "hot things hot enough, cold things cold enough" means.

1. ☐ Bacteria grow quickly when the temperature of food is in the danger zone.

2. ☐ Wash your hands with hot water and soap after you use the rest room.

3. ☐ The food spoiled in the broken refrigerator. The temperature was 75° F.

4. ☐ The fried chicken spoiled in the broken food warmer. The temperature was 75° F.

Step 2: Put a check mark in the box if the sentence shows what *sanitation* means.

1. ☐ Everything that touches food must be sterile, that is, completely free from germs.

2. ☐ Wash your hands with hot water and soap after you use the rest room.

3. ☐ Always smile and be polite because the customer is always right.

4. ☐ Rinse the meat cutting board with a 10 percent bleach solution to kill germs and sterilize it.

Listen and Speak

Step 1: Listen as your teacher reads the two checklists below.

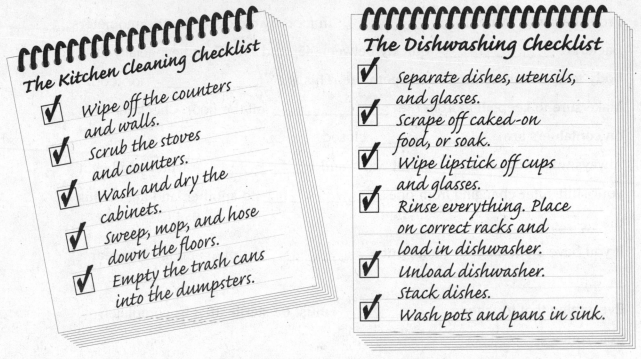

The Kitchen Cleaning Checklist

- ☑ Wipe off the counters and walls.
- ☑ Scrub the stoves and counters.
- ☑ Wash and dry the cabinets.
- ☑ Sweep, mop, and hose down the floors.
- ☑ Empty the trash cans into the dumpsters.

The Dishwashing Checklist

- ☑ Separate dishes, utensils, and glasses.
- ☑ Scrape off caked-on food, or soak.
- ☑ Wipe lipstick off cups and glasses.
- ☑ Rinse everything. Place on correct racks and load in dishwasher.
- ☑ Unload dishwasher. Stack dishes.
- ☑ Wash pots and pans in sink.

Step 2: Now listen as your teacher reads the story about Ty and Sally. They are kitchen workers in a small restaurant.

Today Ty and Sally are cleaning the kitchen. Sally is washing the dishes. Ty is cleaning the stoves, cabinets, and floors.

First, Sally separates the cooking utensils, different-sized plates, and glasses for the dishwasher. Then she soaks the pots and pans in the sink. Next, she wipes lipstick stains off the dirty glasses.

Ty washes the fronts of the cabinets and wipes them dry with another cloth. Then he scrapes the grease and caked-on food off the stoves.

Next Sally rinses everything. She places dirty plates onto different-sized racks. She knows that salad plates go in a different rack from dinner plates. She also puts glasses and utensils onto racks. Sally puts the full racks into the dishwasher.

Ty sweeps the floor. Then he mops the floor and hoses it down with water to be sure it is completely clean.

Sally washes the pots and pans that were soaking in the sink. Next she cleans the sink.

Ty and Sally are almost finished with their shift. Ty takes the trash cans outside to empty them, and Sally unloads the clean dishes in the dishwasher.

Step 3: Work with a partner. Take the roles of Ty and Sally and turn the story into a dialogue. Talk about cleaning the kitchen. Include at least four items from the story in your dialogue.

Step 1: Order the sentences from 1 to 9. Then look at the picture. Circle the sentence that tells what is happening in the picture.

1. ____ Sally unloads the dishwasher.

2. ____ Sally wipes lipstick stains off dirty glasses.

3. ____ Sally puts plates and glasses on different-sized racks.

4. ____ Sally separates the cooking utensils, plates, and glasses.

5. ____ Sally cleans the sink.

6. ____ Sally rinses everything.

7. ____ Sally soaks the pots and pans in the sink.

8. ____ Sally loads full racks into the dishwasher.

9. ____ Sally washes the pots and pans.

Step 2: Read each sentence. Circle *Yes* if the sentence is true. Circle *No* if it is false.

1. Ty and Sally are servers in a small restaurant.	Yes	No
2. Sally rinses everything before loading it in the dishwasher.	Yes	No
3. Sally puts all of the dishes in the same rack.	Yes	No
4. Today Sally scrapes the stove and Ty scrapes the plates.	Yes	No
5. Ty hoses down the floor in order to clean his boots.	Yes	No
6. Ty and Sally clean the kitchen completely to make it sanitary.	Yes	No
7. Sally puts glasses with lipstick stains in the dishwasher.	Yes	No
8. Sally soaks the pots and pans before she washes them.	Yes	No
9. The first thing Ty does is empty the trash cans.	Yes	No

Be a Good Worker

It takes a lot of work in the kitchen to make sure the food is safe. Imagine you are a kitchen worker. Read each item below. Then write about the work that you need to do. The first item is done for you.

1. The floor is dirty. What do you do?

I sweep and mop the floor.

2. The dishes are rinsed. What do you do?

3. There are grease stains on the stove. What do you do?

4. There are lipstick marks on a glass. What do you do?

5. The trash cans are full. What do you do?

6. You just mopped the floor. What do you do?

7. Caked-on food is on the counter. What do you do?

8. The refrigerator temperature is 50° F. What do you do?

9. This bowl of salad should be stored in the walk-in. What do you do?

Remember: Bosses like workers who can direct themselves to do good work. A good worker can look and see what needs to be done, then do it completely and well.

Have Some Fun!

Read the words in the list. Then circle the words in the puzzle.
The words may be horizontal, vertical, or diagonal. They may be backwards.
Can you find them all?

temperature	rinse	responsible	hot
thermometer	scrub	empty	cold
food warmer	scrape	germ	soap
freezer	scraper	bacteria	
sterile	check	spoil	
mop	refrigerator	pail	

T	T	U	C	O	L	D	L	R	Y	R	T
I	E	B	A	C	T	E	R	I	A	E	H
N	A	M	Y	R	A	T	I	N	A	S	E
G	M	S	P	O	I	L	Y	S	Z	P	R
E	E	R	G	E	D	S	H	E	P	O	M
K	C	E	H	C	R	R	C	O	S	N	O
A	R	Z	E	H	C	A	E	R	T	S	M
M	A	E	L	I	R	E	T	S	U	I	E
B	T	E	P	N	I	C	E	U	S	B	T
O	E	R	S	C	R	A	P	E	R	L	E
A	R	F	O	O	D	W	A	R	M	E	R
R	O	T	A	R	E	G	I	R	F	E	R
D	E	M	P	T	Y	O	L	W	A	L	K

Step 1: **Listen as your teacher reads the information about bacteria.**

Bacteria can grow quickly if they have four elements: **temperature, time, moisture,** and **food.** The temperature needs to be in the danger zone, between 45° F and 140° F (7° C and 60° C). The bacteria need enough time for the temperature to rise or fall to the danger zone. Bacteria also need moisture, which is the opposite of dryness. Finally, there needs to be food to feed the bacteria.

Step 2: **Can the food spoil? Read and answer each item below. Two are done for you.**

1. If an apple is on a counter at room temperature for eight hours, can it spoil? Why or why not?

   No, an apple is dry. There is no moisture.

2. A bowl of homemade applesauce is on a kitchen counter for eight hours. The temperature is 80° F. Can the applesauce spoil? Why or why not?

   Yes, that brings all four elements together.

3. A box of raw chicken is in the refrigerator for four hours. The temperature in the refrigerator is 34° F. Can the chicken spoil? Why or why not?

   _____

4. A box of raw chicken is on the kitchen counter for four hours. The temperature is 62° F. Can the chicken spoil? Why or why not?

   _____

5. A box of raw chicken is in a broken refrigerator. The temperature reads 57° F. Can the chicken spoil? Why or why not?

   _____

6. An open bag of chips is on the counter all afternoon. The temperature is 75° F. Can the chips spoil? Why or why not?

   _____

Check Your Understanding

Step 1: Read the question. Circle the best answer.

1. You want to know who is responsible for sweeping, mopping, and hosing down the floor tonight. What do you ask?
   a. What time is it?
   b. Will Charlie be here tonight?
   c. Who is cleaning the floor tonight?

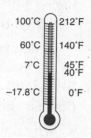

2. You see that the freezer is too warm. You don't know if the boss already knows about the freezer. What do you ask?
   a. Did anyone tell the boss that the freezer is too warm?
   b. Can I take my break now?
   c. Is the freezer too warm?

Step 2: Answer the questions. Write your answers on the lines below.

1. The thermometer in the food warmer reads 85° F. What do you tell the boss?

   _____

2. Your co-worker has a cut on his hand and no bandage on it. What do you say?

   _____

3. You see some raw fish on the counter and you want to know how long

   it has been there. What do you ask your co-worker? _____

   _____

4. You want to find out if your co-worker has washed and sterilized the

   cutting boards. What do you ask your co-worker?_____

   _____

Complete three of the activities below. Write your answers on other paper.

1. What does "hot things hot enough, cold things cold enough" mean to you? On another piece of paper, write your answer in a paragraph.

2. Work with a small group. Make a list of the food-safety rules you learned in this unit. Discuss these questions:
   - Which of the rules can you also follow at home?
   - Which rules do you think are most important?

3. Work with a partner. Talk with a partner about ways that food can spoil. Discuss these questions:
   - Why do some foods need to stay in a cold refrigerator?
   - Why do some foods need to stay in a food warmer?
   - Why are dry foods safe from bacteria?

4. Have you or anyone you know ever had experience with food poisoning? Talk with a partner about experiences with food that was not safe to eat.

5. Why is it important for restaurants to be sanitary? Write your answer in a paragraph.

Notes

_____

_____

_____

_____

_____

Read the words in the box. Underline any words you don't know.
Then look at the picture. What are the people in the picture doing?

Words to Know:

nobody	must	(to) cover the	
o'clock	(to) act	floor	promptly
owner	(to) be late	(to) have to	yet
schedule	(to) be off	(to) notify	
somebody	(to) be promoted	(to) trade	having car
supervisor	(to) call in	(to) work for	trouble
toothache	(to) clock in/out		I'm not sure.
	(to) cover for	careful	See you later.
		valid	

Listen and Speak

Step 1:   Listen as your teacher reads the dialogue.

David: I usually feel fine, but I can't finish my shift today. I have a
bad toothache, and I have to go to the dentist immediately.

Lily: Oh, I'm sorry to hear that. Did you tell Lee?

David: Lee? She's a server. Why Lee?

Lily: Lee was promoted to manager trainee. She's the acting manager today.

David: Oh. Well, you're right. I have to tell her.

Lily: Yes. We always have to tell the supervisor promptly if we have a
valid reason to be out. Who will work for you when you go?

David: I don't know. Maybe nobody.

Lily: Somebody has to work for you. Well, I'm off work now.
I can trade shifts with you. You can work for me next week, OK?
Let's tell Lee now. Wait a minute, I have to answer the phone.
Hello, Las Flores Restaurant. May I help you?

Teresa: Hi, Lily. This is Teresa. I'm going to be late today. I'm having car trouble.

Lily: OK. I'll tell Lee. She is the acting manager today. What time will you
be here?

Teresa: I'm not sure. I'll call again if it will be after five o'clock.

Lily: OK. See you later. I can tell Lee in a few minutes. Good-bye.

LATER

David: Lee, I have a bad toothache and have to leave for the dentist now.
Lily is going to trade shifts with me. I'll work for her next Tuesday.
Can you change the schedule for us?

Lee: OK. I'm sorry about your emergency, but it's good that Lily can cover
for you. Be sure to clock out before you go.

Lily: But Lee, there's another problem. Teresa called in with car trouble.
She'll be late.

Lee: Well, I'll have to cover for her. We have to cover the floor and serve
the customers. Let's get busy.

Step 2:   Work in a group of four students. Read the dialogue.

Step 3:   Discuss these questions with your group.
- David and Teresa have problems, so they can't work.
  How do they handle the situation?
- Do you think it is OK for David and Teresa to miss work? Why?
- When do you think it is OK to miss work?

Practice

Step 1: Read each sentence. Circle *Yes* if the sentence is true and *No* if it is false.

1. David and Lily manage a restaurant.	Yes	No
2. Lee can finish her own shift.	Yes	No
3. David has to go to the doctor today.	Yes	No
4. Lee tells David to go to the dentist.	Yes	No
5. Lily will trade shifts and cover for David.	Yes	No
6. Lily and Lee will cover the floor.	Yes	No
7. 'Cover the floor' means mop the floor.	Yes	No

Step 2: Circle the picture that shows a real emergency, a valid excuse to miss work.

1.

"My baby is sick."

2.

"I need my annual checkup."

Step 3: Read the sentences. Put a check mark in the box next to the sentences that show valid reasons for missing work.

1. ❏ You stayed up late last night. Now you can't get out of bed.
2. ❏ Your car has a flat tire.
3. ❏ Your child had an accident at school. You need to take your child to the doctor.
4. ❏ You fell down and hurt your ankle. The doctor says you shouldn't walk.
5. ❏ You need to go to the telephone company and pay your phone bill.
6. ❏ You are tired, and you would rather stay home and read a book.
7. ❏ You want to take the test to get your driver's license.
8. ❏ Your sister is getting married.
9. ❏ You want to go to a concert.
10. ❏ You have a fever.

Build Your Vocabulary

Words to Know:

breakfast shift		A.M. (before noon)	closing time
dinner shift	(to) let out	P.M. (after noon)	for the most part
lunch shift	(to) start	sleepy	keep busy
night shift			personal business
split shift			time off

Step 1: Teresa is a server at a restaurant. She has to work one split shift and one night shift a week. Read what Teresa says about her shifts.

"I like to work the breakfast shift. This is my favorite shift. Customers come in sleepy, but they leave happy. The lunch shift is good, too. The customers are in a hurry, and I always keep busy.

"On a split shift, I work between 11:00 A.M. and 2:00 P.M. for lunch. I have time off between 2:00 P.M. and 5:00 P.M. to take care of personal business. Then I work again from 5:00 P.M. to 9:00 P.M. for dinner. In the evening, families come in to eat together. They are very nice customers, for the most part.

"Once a week, I work the night shift. It gets slow after dinner. Then it gets busy again at 9:30 P.M. People come in for a snack after the movies let out."

Step 2: Answer the questions about Teresa's job.

1. Which shift is Teresa's favorite shift? Why?

_____

2. Which shift do you think is best? Why?

_____

_____

Step 1: Read the story about Teresa's work schedule.

Teresa's Schedule

Monday	**Thursday**
6:00 A.M.–2:00 P.M.	8:00 P.M.–2:00 A.M.
Tuesday	**Friday**
11:00 A.M.–2:00 P.M.	1:00 P.M.–9:00 P.M.
5:00 P.M.–9:00 P.M.	
	Saturday
Wednesday	1:00 P.M.–9:00 P.M.
Off	
	Sunday
	Off

On Monday Teresa works the breakfast shift. She starts at six o'clock in the morning and finishes at two o'clock in the afternoon. It's an eight-hour shift.

On Tuesday Teresa works a split shift. She starts at eleven o'clock in the morning and finishes the first part of her shift at two o'clock in the afternoon. She has time off between two o'clock and five o'clock. Teresa can go to see the dentist on Tuesday at three o-clock.

At five o'clock, she starts working again. She finishes at nine o'clock at night. It's a seven-hour shift.

This week Teresa doesn't work on Wednesday or on Sunday. These are her days off. She does prefer to have her days off come together, though.

On Thursday Teresa starts at eight o'clock at night. It's the end of the dinner shift. She finishes at two o'clock in the morning, closing time. It's a six-hour shift.

Teresa works the same shift on Friday and Saturday. She works from one o'clock in the afternoon until nine o'clock at night. These are eight-hour shifts.

Step 2: Circle True if the statement is true and False if it is false.

1. Teresa prefers to have her days off come together. **True** **False**

2. Teresa works the breakfast shift on Thursday. **True** **False**

3. Teresa works seven–hour shifts on Friday and Saturday. **True** **False**

4. Teresa gets a three-hour break when she works a split shift. **True** **False**

5. Teresa's long shifts are on Monday, Friday, and Saturday. **True** **False**

Listen and Speak

Step 1: Listen as your teacher reads the dialogue.

David: I made a big mistake. I left the fruit pies on the counter last night. I forgot to put them in the refrigerator. I'm afraid to tell Tony because maybe he'll fire me.

Lee: Well, you have to tell Tony. He's a good manager, and I don't think he'll fire you. Let's talk about *how* to tell him.

David: Thanks.

Lee: How do you feel about this mistake? Are you sorry?

David: Yeah. I'm really sorry. I'll never do that again.

Lee: So you can say, "I apologize. It won't happen again."

David: Yeah, I'll remember from now on and be more careful next time, too.

Lee: You could say that, too.

LATER

Tony: That's really a serious error. We could get vermin in here. The Health Department could close us down.

David: I know. You're right. It was a big mistake.

Tony: I'm glad you realize that.

David: I apologize. It won't happen again. I'll be more careful from now on.

Tony: That's good to hear. You're usually a good worker. I know you try hard. I'm glad you talked to me about it. It shows that you're responsible.

David: Thank you, Tony. I won't do it again.

Tony: I know you won't. Don't worry about it any more. Let's forget about it.

Words to Know:

bookkeeper	(to) fire
error	(to) worry
Health Department	
pay period	afraid
vermin	responsible
	forget about it
could	good to hear
(to) feel	next time

Step 2: Read the dialogue with two other students.

Step 3: Discuss these questions.
- What was David's mistake? Why was it a mistake?
- What do you think vermin are? Why are vermin a problem?
- Did David handle the situation the right way? Why?

Step 1: **Fill in the following sentences from the conversation on page 102.**

Tony: That's really a serious _____. We could get _____ in

here. The Health Department could close us down.

David: I know. You're right. It was a big _____.

Tony: I'm glad you _____ that.

David: I apologize. It won't happen again. I'll be more _____ from now on.

Tony: That's good to hear. You're usually a good worker. I know you

_____ hard. I'm glad you _____ to me about it.

It shows you're _____.

David: Thank you, Tony. I won't do it _____.

Tony: I know you won't. Don't _____ _____

_____ anymore. Let's _____ _____

_____.

Step 2: **Draw a line from the mistake to the letter of the correct solution.
The first one is done for you.**

1. Uh-oh! I forgot to do that.
2. Uh-oh! I didn't clean that
   well enough.
3. Uh-oh! I broke that.
4. Uh-oh! I burned that toast.
5. Uh-oh! I didn't finish that important job.
6. Uh-oh! I spilled water on the floor.
7. Uh-oh! I forgot to give my customer
   more coffee.

a. I'll clean it up before someone slips
and falls.

b. I should have checked on it.

c. I'll work on it some more right now.

d. I'll remember to do it next time.

e. I should have done the more important
job first and the other one afterward.

f. I'll take some to my customer now.

g. I'll be more careful from now on.

Be a Good Worker

Step 1: It is important for a worker to plan ahead and give the manager notice of special scheduling needs. Practice these sentences with a partner:

Worker: I have to go to a wedding two weeks from Saturday. Can you please schedule me off on that day?

Manager: Of course. Thanks for the notice.

Worker: There's been a death in the family, and I must go to a funeral. It will be tomorrow afternoon. Can I get time off?

Manager: I'll see if somebody can trade with you, or maybe we can work shorthanded. I'll do my best to find someone. I'll let you know shortly.

Worker: My son was named Student of the Month. There's a ceremony I'd like to attend next Wednesday morning.

Manager: I can schedule you to come in at eleven o'clock next Wednesday. Would that help?

Step 2: Giving enough notice is very important for scheduling. Workers should give a supervisor plenty of notice or schedule appointments for a day off. Does the worker give enough notice in the examples below? Write "enough notice" or "not enough notice" in the space after each item.

1. Mona makes a doctor's appointment for this afternoon and asks for today off.

   This is _____.

2. Gerardo wants to attend his graduation. He asks for the day off in four weeks.

   This is _____.

3. Mark wants to take his mother to the dentist for oral surgery. He asks for tomorrow off.

   This is _____.

4. Elvira wants to take her son to the ice show for his birthday. She asks for the day off six weeks in advance. This is _____.

5. Miriam makes a doctor's appointment for a week from Friday. She asks for the day off.

   This is _____.

Have Some Fun!

Write the correct words from the box on the lines below. Then complete the puzzle.

car	trouble	have to
fire	cover	careful
schedule	trade	valid
shift	has to	

Across

2. My _____ has a flat tire.

3. If you _____ shifts, you work for someone and he or she works for you.

4. I _____ tell the manager if I'm sick.

6. I can't finish my _____ today.

7. Call in if you have a _____ excuse.

8. I'm afraid Tony will _____ me.

Down

1. I'll be more _____ from now on.

2. We have to _____ the floor.

4. David _____ leave early.

5. Teresa is having car _____.

6. I can _____ you to come in later.

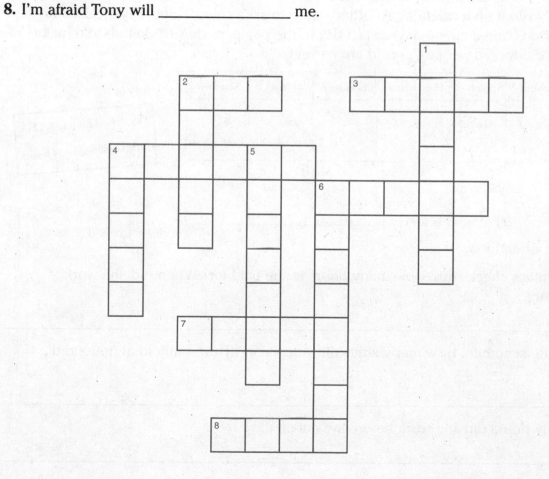

Think It Over

Read each story. Then complete the exercise that follows.

The Time Clock

Most restaurants use time clocks to keep track of everybody's working time. A worker must "clock in" when starting a shift and "clock out" when finishing a shift. That way, the bookkeeper knows how much to pay a worker for each pay period.

Circle the picture that shows the worker clocking in.

1.

2.

Pay Periods

A worker should keep track of the time he or she works. One way to keep track of time is to write it on a calendar. Another way is to save check stubs. Paychecks show the "pay period" and a cut-off day, or last day in the pay period. A worker should make sure the hours worked per pay period are correct.

SUNDAY	MONDAY	TUESDAY	WEDNESDAY	THURSDAY	FRIDAY	SATURDAY
5 Joe 9-5	6 Alice 9-5	7 ALice 9-5	8 Joe 9-5	9	10 Joe 9-5 Julia 5-1 A.M.	11 Joe 9-5 Julia 5-1 A.M.
12 Julia 4-12 Cut Off Day	13	14 Julia 5-1 A.M.	15	16 Julia 5-1 A.M.	17 Pay Day	18

> Pay Period Ending 5-12
>
> Julia Godlewski - 24 hours

Answer the questions.

1. Look at Julia's check stub. How many hours is she paid for? When did she work those hours?

_____

2. Look at the schedule. How many shifts did Alice work? How many total hours did she work?

_____

3. How many hours did Joe work before the cut-off day?

_____

Check Your Understanding

Step 1: Sometimes a worker has a problem with a paycheck. The worker has to talk to the manager about the problem. Binh is sure that he was underpaid for the last pay period. Read the conversation below. Then practice it with a partner.

Binh: I know I worked six eight-hour shifts in the last pay period. I worked Monday through Saturday, but I only got paid for five days.

Tony: Your timecard says that you were off on Thursday.

Binh: No, I worked for José on Thursday. I was here working with you, do you remember?

Tony: Actually, I do remember you helping me with our Thursday inventory. But your timecard doesn't show that you worked.

Binh: Oh, maybe I forgot to clock in. What should I do? We both know that I worked.

Tony: We have to talk to the bookkeeper. Clocking in and out proves that you worked. It tells the time that you began and ended your shift.

Step 2: Susan is confused about why her first paycheck is so small, so she asks her manager about it. Read Tony and Susan's conversation with a partner.

Susan: I don't understand, Tony. I have worked here since last Wednesday. I worked five days, but I only got paid for three days! Here are the shifts that I worked.

Tony: That's because our cut-off day is Sunday. You worked three days—Wednesday, Thursday, and Friday. You had two days off, and then you worked on Monday and Tuesday. You get paid for the time you worked before the cut-off day.

Wed., Thurs., Fri.: 7:00-3:00
Sat., Sun.: Off
Mon., Tues.: 6:00-2:00

Susan: Oh, I get it. That means that *next* payday I'll get paid for the other days, right?

Tony: Right.

Step 3: Work with a partner to answer the questions below. Write your answers on another sheet of paper.
- Why is it important to clock in and clock out at work?
- What is a pay period?
- What is a cut-off day?

Complete the activities below. Write your answers on other paper.

1. Work with a small group of students. Talk about food-service jobs that are good for students. Discuss these questions:

   • Would you like to work full time or part time? Why?

   • Which shift would be better for you—breakfast shift, lunch shift, dinner shift, night shift, or split shift? Why?

2. Work with a partner. Make a list of valid reasons for taking time off work. You and your partner must agree that the reasons are valid. Present your list of reasons to the class.

3. Write a note to your supervisor. Ask for a day off in the future. Explain why you need the day off. Remember, you should use a valid reason to take time off.

Notes

_____

_____

_____

_____

_____

_____

_____

Unit 10
A NEW MANAGER

Read the words in the box. Underline any words you don't know.
Then look at the picture. Who are the people? What are they doing?

Words to Know:

advertising	position	(to) assign	(to) study
aspects	promotion	(to) balance	
authority	public relations	(to) delegate	challenging
bank	purchasing	(to) be accounted for	enthusiastic
budgeting	receipts		exciting
business	salary	(to) be excited about	hourly
deposit	skills		
finances	staff	(to) be familiar with	around
input	the house		
inventory	workshops	(to) leave	work your way up
money		(to) remind	
morale		(to) share	

Listen and Speak

Step 1: **Listen as your teacher reads the dialogue.**

Tony: I want to congratulate you on your promotion to manager trainee.

Lee: Thank you. I'm excited about my new position.

Tony: It's good that you've worked your way up in the business. You know all aspects of our operation.

Lee: Yes. I'm familiar with the jobs in the back of the house and in the front of the house. So I can cover for someone in the kitchen or in the dining room.

Tony: Good. You're not an hourly employee any more. Managers are paid a salary to get the job done, but we should not do everything ourselves. We have to delegate authority. That means that we have to assign work to others and then check on their progress.

Lee: I think I'll need to practice delegating. I have no experience doing that.

Tony: I'll be giving you the schedule for your training workshops. You'll have to study purchasing, advertising, keeping inventory, and public relations.

Lee: It all sounds exciting and challenging.

Tony: You'll also have to meet with our bookkeeper to learn about finances and budgeting. And you'll go to the bank to learn how to make deposits.

Lee: I'm looking forward to it! I like to learn new skills.

Tony: Speaking of money, I want you to look at the cash receipts when the cashier balances the money. Also, can you think of ways to remind the staff not to leave money around? All the money needs to be accounted for.

Lee: I already have an idea about that to share with you later.

Tony: Excellent! I want your input.

Lee: Great.

Tony: It's a pleasure to work with such a capable and enthusiastic trainee. I know you will keep the staff morale high.

Lee: Thank you!

Tony: You're welcome.

Step 2: **Read the dialogue with a partner.**

Step 1: Write *T* in the space if the sentence is true.
Write *F* if the sentence is false.

_____ 1. Tony congratulates Lee on her promotion.

_____ 2. Lee is nervous about her new position.

_____ 3. Lee has worked her way up in the food service business.

_____ 4. Lee is familiar with all aspects of the operation of a restaurant.

_____ 5. Managers never have to cover when employees are absent.

_____ 6. Lee has a lot of practice in delegating authority.

_____ 7. Lee is looking forward to learning new skills.

_____ 8. Lee will learn about purchasing.

_____ 9. The restaurant has a bookkeeper.

_____ 10. Lee will learn how to make deposits at the bank.

_____ 11. The staff leaves money around.

_____ 12. Tony wants all the money accounted for.

_____ 13. Lee has no input for Tony about how the staff should handle money.

_____ 14. Tony doesn't want Lee's input.

_____ 15. Tony is happy about having Lee as a manager trainee.

Step 2: Read each item. Write your answers in the spaces below.

1. The front of the house is the area where the customers go. The back of the house is where the food is prepared and the offices are. Where in the house would you prefer to work? Why?

_____

_____

_____

2. Do you think Lee will be a good manager? Why or why not?

_____

_____

_____

Build Your Vocabulary

Step 1: A manager has many responsibilities. Study the pictures and read the statements about those responsibilities.

Words to Know:

case	(to) interview
decision	(to) reprimand
emergency	(to) request
(to) compliment	private
(to) hire	

"I think we can solve this problem easily."

"Let's order six cases next time."

"Let's see. David said he needs Monday off."

Step 2: Work with a partner. Read each situation below and discuss it with your partner. Circle the situation if you agree with the manager's response.

1. A customer slips and hurts himself. The manager says, "You should have been more careful."

2. A customer yells at a server. The manager tells the server, "We have to be polite even if the customer isn't."

3. A server requests a day off. The manager says, "I'm the boss and I say you don't need a day off."

4. There are ketchup, mustard, and oil spills on the kitchen counter. The manager says, "Be sure to scrub the counter. We need to keep the kitchen clean at all times."

Practice

Step 1:   Circle *Yes* if the statement is true and *No* if it is false.

1. A manager has to make decisions.   **Yes**   **No**

2. A manager is responsible for the safety of employees and customers.   **Yes**   **No**

3. A manager schedules employees' work hours.   **Yes**   **No**

4. A manager has to solve problems and make things run smoothly.   **Yes**   **No**

5. A manager should try to do everything without help.   **Yes**   **No**

Step 2:   Read the paragraph carefully. Then write your answers to the questions below.

Sometimes a manager has to hire a new worker. The manager has to interview the person and find out about his or her experience. Sometimes a manager compliments a worker who has done an excellent job. Sometimes a manager has to reprimand an employee. This should always be done in private. Sometimes a manager has to fire a worker. This can happen when a worker breaks the rules or doesn't do his or her job. Firing a worker is a difficult part of a manager's job.

1. Who interviews new employees?

_____

2. How should a manager reprimand an employee?

_____

3. When should a manager give compliments?

_____

4. When should a manager fire an employee?

_____

5. Would you like to be a manager? Why or why not?

_____

Listen and Speak

Step 1: Listen as your teacher reads the dialogue.

Lee: Congratulations, Max. You're going to be our next Employee of the Month!

Max: No kidding!

Lee: Yes. It's true! You were selected because of your positive attitude and your high standards of work performance.

Max: Thank you. Will my name and picture be on the wall?

Lee: That's right. And you will get a special award to take home. Congratulations again. So how do you like your job?

Max: At first I thought I'd just work here temporarily. Lately I've been thinking about making a career in the food-service business.

Lee: Do you want to go into management?

Max: Actually, I think I'd like to go to culinary school to be a chef or maybe learn how to cater. I think I might even like to own a catering business one day. What about you? What made you want to be a manager?

Lee: Being Employee of the Month first gave me the idea that I could be a manager myself.

Max: Is being a manager your final goal?

Lee: Someday I'd like to own my own restaurant. There are lots of opportunities in this business for hard-working, motivated, responsible workers—lots of opportunities.

Max: I hope so! Oh, congratulations on your promotion.

Lee: Thank you, and congratulations again to you, too.

Words to Know:	
career	(to) be selected
catering	(to) cater
communication	(to) own
congratulations	
employee	culinary
goal	final
graduate	motivated
management	own
opportunities	positive
performance	
standards	temporarily
	No kidding!

Step 2: Read the dialogue with a partner.

Step 3: Discuss the questions below.
- Why is Max going to be the Employee of the Month?
- Lee was an Employee of the Month. How did it help her?
- What goals do Max and Lee share?

Employee	picture	award	business	responsible
culinary	standards	opportunities	catering	chef
kidding	attitude	promotion	career	congratulations
Month	motivated	restaurant		

Step 1: Choose from the words above to fill the blanks.

1. Lee says _____ to Max and tells him he is going to be the next _____ of the Month.

2. Max was selected because of his positive _____ and his high _____ of performance.

3. Max says, "No _____," when Lee tells him that he is going to be Employee of the _____.

4. Max will get a special _____ to take home, and his name and _____ will be on the restaurant wall.

5. Max wants to make a _____ in the food-service _____.

6. Max is thinking about going to _____ school to be a _____ or to learn how to cater.

7. Max might like to open his own _____ business one day.

8. Lee wants to own her own _____ someday.

9. Lee says that there are lots of _____ for hard-working, _____, and _____ workers.

10. Max congratulates Lee on her _____.

Step 2: Answer the questions. Write your answers in the spaces below.

1. What opportunities are there in the food service business? _____
_____

2. Give some examples of a positive attitude. _____
_____

Be a Good Worker

Step 1: Read the following statements about the Employee of the Month.

The Employee of the Month:

· is always polite and helpful and gets along well with co-workers and supervisors.

· is a good team player and always cooperates with others.

· follows safety and sanitation rules.

· reports on time, has a good attendance record, and takes breaks as scheduled.

· has a good attitude, is motivated and self-directed, and takes responsibility for his or her own actions.

· leaves personal issues at home and does not spend working time on non-business matters.

Step 2: Put a check mark next to the statements that tell what a good worker does.

A good worker:

1. ____ is polite to customers and co-workers.

2. ____ has good attendance.

3. ____ has a good attitude.

4. ____ apologizes to customers if necessary.

5. ____ knows about safety and sanitation.

6. ____ tries to do good work.

7. ____ takes lots of breaks.

8. ____ produces good quality work.

9. ____ informs supervisor of absence.

10. ____ does his or her best.

11. ____ breaks the rules.

12. ____ helps customers.

13. ____ smiles at customers.

14. ____ works as part of a team.

15. ____ takes breaks as scheduled.

16. ____ is responsible.

17. ____ is hardworking.

18. ____ leaves personal business at home.

Have Some Fun!

congratulations	schedule	exciting	hire	inventory
promotion	month	career	money	decisions
staff	chef	business	compliment	culinary
input	job	opportunities	supervisor	remind
bank	motivated	manager	cater	deposit
bookkeeper	management	goal	fire	own

The words in the box are in the puzzle below. Find them and circle them.
The words may fit horizontally, vertically, or diagonally. They may be backwards.
Can you find them all?

C	B	U	S	I	N	E	S	S	R	M	O	N	E	Y	O
O	R	O	C	B	O	C	N	O	I	T	O	M	O	R	P
M	R	O	O	U	O	C	A	R	E	E	R	A	J	O	P
C	G	M	H	K	L	J	H	T	F	H	O	N	G	T	O
O	U	O	A	T	K	I	D	E	E	I	S	A	N	N	R
M	D	T	A	N	N	E	N	N	F	R	I	G	I	E	T
P	E	I	U	L	A	O	E	A	I	E	V	E	T	V	U
L	P	V	N	P	B	G	M	P	R	M	R	R	I	N	N
I	O	A	S	T	N	A	E	O	E	Y	E	P	C	I	I
M	S	T	A	F	F	I	S	M	T	R	P	R	X	N	T
E	I	E	C	I	O	S	C	H	E	D	U	L	E	W	I
N	T	D	D	E	C	I	S	I	O	N	S	R	S	O	E
T	C	O	N	G	R	A	T	U	L	A	T	I	O	N	S

Think It Over

Step 1: Read the information about communication skills.

A successful manager has good communication skills. A manager should be understanding and polite to workers.

Lee knows how to talk to employees. When she makes a request, she is polite and uses the employee's name. The employees know who is in charge, so she doesn't have to speak loudly or be mean. When Lee makes everyday requests, she uses the words *could* or *would*.

Step 2: You're the manager. Read the sentences below. Use your communication skills to complete the questions.

1. You want a worker to empty the trash cans in the kitchen. Ask, "Could you

   _____?"

2. You want a worker to bring out some clean glasses. Ask, "Would you

   _____?"

3. You want a worker to get a high chair for a customer. Ask, "Would you

   _____?"

4. You think there should be more fruit on the serving line. Ask, "Could you

   _____?"

5. You want a worker to refill the condiments. Ask, "Would you

   _____?"

Check Your Understanding

You're the manager. Respond to the situations below.
Write your responses on the lines.

1. You want to congratulate a co-worker on his or her promotion.

   _____

   _____

2. You want an employee to fill the salt and pepper shakers.

   _____

   _____

3. You see some spilled liquid on the floor. You want Joe to mop it up.

   _____

   _____

4. An employee calls to say he'll be late. You want another employee to cover for him.

   _____

   _____

5. You want a kitchen worker to wipe off the counters.

   _____

   _____

6. You want to know if a customer would like some more coffee.

   _____

   _____

7. You want to tell an employee that he or she has to arrive at work on time.

   _____

   _____

8. An employee asks to take time off to take her sick baby to the doctor.

   _____

   _____

9. An employee asks to take time off to go to the movies.

   _____

   _____

Complete four of the activities below. Write your answers on other paper.

1. Talk to a partner about careers in food service. Which careers interest you? On another piece of paper, write a few sentences about each job to explain why you are interested in the job.

2. What are the qualities of a good worker? Write them in a list.

3. What does "working your way up" mean? Write a paragraph to explain your answer. Include examples from food-service jobs.

4. Research culinary schools in your area. Answer these questions:
   - What courses of study does each school offer?
   - Does the school help graduates get jobs? What kinds of jobs can graduates get?
   - How much does it cost to attend these schools?

5. You are a restaurant manager. You have to delegate work. How can you make sure that the work gets done? Write your answer in a paragraph.

6. Work with a partner. Talk about what makes a good manager. Discuss these questions:
   - What strengths should a good manager have?
   - What does a good manager do when an employee gets hurt?
   - What does a good manager say to angry customers?

Notes

_____

_____

_____

_____

_____

Words to Know

Pay attention, 73
Pay period, 102, 106
Pepper, 4
Pepperoni, 18
Performance, 114
Personal business, 100
Phone number, 18
Pick-up, 18
Pick up, 18
Pickle, 1
Picture, 115
Pie, 9
Pin, 78
Pitcher, 37
Pizza, 18
Place, 76
Place setting, 38
Plastic wrap, 88
Plate, 4
Please, 1
P.M., 100
Polite, 6
Popular, 30
Portion, 64
Position, 109
Positive, 114
Potato cheese soup, 61
Potato skins, 30
Pots, 73
Poultry, 88
Pour, 64
Prepare, 25
Price, 6
Private, 112
Probably, 49
Problem, 30
Promotion, 109
Promptly, 97
Proud, 64
Pry open, 76
Public relations, 109
Pull, 78, 79
Purchasing, 109
Put out, 78

Q

Quickly, 78

R

Ranch, 25
Rare, 25, 27
Raw, 88
Reach-in, 85
Reading, 85
Ready, 13
Receipts, 109
Recommend, 30
Refill, 6, 66
Refrigerator, 85
Relax, 28
Relish, 13

Remember, 37
Remind, 109, 117
Repeat, 13
Replace, 66
Report, 73
Reprimand, 112
Request, 112
Reservation, 49
Reserve, 49
Responsibility, 85
Responsible, 102, 115
Rest room, 88
Restaurant, 1
Rhyme, 37
Rice, 25
Rice pilaf, 30
Right, 37
Right away, 16
Right here, 49
Right this way, 49
Right with you, 49
Rinse, 88
Roast beef, 13
Roll, 28
Room, 88
Rules, 73
Run out of, 64
Run smoothly, 52
Rush, 25

S

Safety, 73
Safety rules, 74, 76, 79
Salad, 1
Salad dressing, 25, 27
    blue cheese, 25, 27
    Italian, 25, 27
    low fat, 25, 27
    ranch, 25, 27
    Thousand Island, 25, 27
Salad fork, 40, 41
Salad plate, 40, 41
Salary, 109
Salt, 4
Salt and pepper
    shakers, 40, 41
Salty, 30
Sandwich, 1
Sanitation, 88
Sanitize, 88
Satisfied, 16
Sauce, 25
Saucer, 37, 40, 41
Sausage, 18
Schedule, 97
Scrape, 88, 93
Scraper, 93
Scrub, 88, 93
Seat, 49, 52
See, 25
See you later, 97
Separate, 66, 88

Serve, 25
Server, 25
Service, 28
Serving line, 61
Set the table, 37
Set up, 37
Shakers, 37
Share, 109
Sharp, 76
Shift, 73, 97, 100
    breakfast, 100
    dinner, 100
    lunch, 100
    night, 100
    split, 100
Show, 37
Side order, 1
Side work, 66, 70
Sign, 73
Silverware, 37
Sir, 42
Situation, 30
Size, 1
Skills, 109
Sleepy, 100
Slicer, 76
Slices, 18
Slip, 73
Slippery, 73
Small, 1
Smell, 78
Smile, 6
Smoke alarm, 78
Smoking, 49
Smother, 78
Sneeze guard, 66
Soap, 88
Soda, 1
Soft drink, 1
Solve, 30
Somebody, 97
Someday, 42
Soon, 37
Sound good, 61
Soup, 25
Soup du jour, 61
Soupspoon, 40, 41
Sour cream, 25
Special, 25
Spell, 49
Spill, 73
Split pea soup, 61
Split shift, 100
Spoil, 85
Spoon, 1
Squeeze, 78, 79
Stack, 88
Staff, 109
Standards, 114
Start, 100
Station, 37
Stay, 85
Stay even, 64

Steak, 25
Steak knife, 41
Steam table, 64
Sterile, 88
Sterilize, 88
Sticky, 66
Stir, 64
Stir stick, 4
Store, 73
Stove, 78
Straw, 1
Strawberry shortcake, 30
Study, 109
Succeed, 64
Sugar, 4
Sugar bowl, 40, 41
Supervisor, 97
Supposed to, 85
Sure, 54
Sweep, 88
Sweeping motion, 78, 79

T

T-bone, 25
Table settings, 38
Take back, 30
Take out, 2
Tax, 1
Tea, 1
Team, 37
Teaspoon, 40, 41
Telling time, 56, 58
Temperature, 64
Temporarily, 114
Thank you, 1
That will be about . . ., 18
That's all, 13
There's, 37
Thermometer, 64, 86
They're, 37
Thick, 18
Think so, 73
Thousand Island, 25
Throw away, 85
Tightly, 88
Time, on clocks, 56, 58
Time Clock, 106
Time off, 100
Tip, 28
Tomatoes, 13
Tonight, 25
Toothache, 97
Toothpicks, 66
Topping, 18
Trade, 97
Trainee, 61
Training, 64
Tray, 6
Trouble, 105
Try, 30
Try It!, 12, 23
Turn off, 73